The Flip Side of Flipping

The Easier Way to Real Estate Riches

by *The***Wolff** *Couple*
Brian & Lynette

with

Ron LeGrand

©TheWolffCouple.com   888-Rich-Now

Get Your **FREE** Bonuses!

Download the Audiobook
PLUS
Get Our Money-Making Report
"Fast Steps to Pretty House Profits"
($197 Value)

"Our Mission is Your Success", so to keep you motivated and on track we want to give you these amazing Gifts absolutely **FREE**! You will LOVE the Audiobook, featuring **the Wolffs AND Ron LeGrand!**
The powerful Report will help get you going fast.
Go to the Website below to claim your FREE Bonuses!

Just go to **InvestingGift.com** and
Use the Special Access Code **FSF1011**

About The Cover For
"THE FLIP SIDE OF FLIPPING"

We started off with one main idea for the cover, and a hundred ideas for the cover. The main idea, the one "must" in our minds, was that the cover had to be **perfect**. To us, this subject matter deserved perfection. This book was all about Creative Financing, which had made us rich, and had made countless numbers of our students rich. We felt this would be the first book to truly capture all the secrets and systems that lead to "Pretty House" success. This is the subject we've devoted the last 15 years of our lives to teaching, from hundreds of stages to thousands of students, in cities all across our great country.

In our minds, "The Flip Side of Flipping" was destined to be the most ground-breaking real estate investing book since Robert Allen's "Nothing Down" in 1980*. We've always thrived by expecting a lot from ourselves, in fact Brian's long-held motto is *"Expect Success!"* We also have the highest expectation for all of our training materials, and our first book had to be the *pinnacle* of all those efforts. And while the most important part of this book is the money-making content inside, you just can't underestimate the impact of the cover. It's the face of the book, the outstretched hand that helps the vital messages inside find their audience. The cover reaches out with life- changing instruction, reaching out to the most people, and the people who need it the most. It helps change investors' lives for the better.

So what could be the perfect visual representation of Creative Financing, which flips the normal real estate investing model upside down? It enables an investor to pay top price for a home, using no money or credit, and still make a big profit. The elements we needed to incorporate were real estate (more specifically houses), the investing model being flipped, and the resulting real estate riches.

Brian may have graduated Summa Cum Laude, but this was tricky!

Ideas swirled in our heads – a flipping coin, an ugly house as a "mirror image" to a pretty house, twisted arrows, inverted letters, yet nothing we tried captured it. Then one special dawn it hit Brian. It didn't take long to collect house-shaped "piggy" banks, and then choose the best -- a beautiful wooden bank with gold metal trim.

Then it was simply a matter of posing and snapping at precisely the right angle, and we had the picture that would grace the cover of our first book! Our one main idea was realized, it captured "The Flip Side of Flipping" in one memorable image, and it was **perfect!**

*When we met Robert it ended with a 3-way hug & him exclaiming

"I love you guys!"

Table of Contents

From the Wolff Couple to YOU!

Wherever you are in your life, you now have the p_ower to change your future. How many times have you gotten psyched up to succeed, filled with enthusiasm, but then were left without a real vehicle to reach your dreams? As of this moment right now you can never say you didn't find that vehicle, because you found this ground-breaking book. We found Ron LeGrand, and now you found us!

Here are the secrets AND the detailed systems you need to grow rich using Creative Financing. Yes, you can follow the proven scripts & systems right here to achieve your financial goals and
CHANGE YOUR LIFE!
Now it's up to you -- on your exciting journey ahead, always keep in mind our all-important m_ottoes:

"EXPECT SUCCESS!"

"TAKE ACTION!"

Dedication

This book is dedicated to all those dreamers out there, all those **outside-the-box thinkers** who are on a path that has now linked up with ours. This book is dedicated to all those who **take a chance on themselves** and TAKE ACTION! This is dedicated to all those investors of the future who are about to make **an act of faith** today by buying and reading this book. This is dedicated to all those who will use this book as **a starting point to a new life** for themselves and their loved ones. We hope **this book is dedicated to YOU!**

We also dedicate this book to **Ron LeGrand**, we wouldn't be here without our *great friend and Mentor!*

We've been blessed to have had an exciting and lucrative career as Real Estate Investors, and there was one definite turning point. We met **Ron LeGrand** over 15 years ago, and he absolutely **changed our lives** forever.

Ron's bought **over 3000 homes**, and he's still investing today. More than **half a million people** have attended his trainings, and he's the **nation's leading authority** on Creative Financing House Deals. Folks love Ron for his **"straight-shooting"** Southern style, and admire him for his expertise on all things Real Estate.

He's the man who first showed us **the path to success through Creative Financing ("Pretty House") Deals!**

Ron's been our Mentor, and we've grown to be great friends. We've cruised with him & Bev (wonderful wife of 52 years) to Hawaii, Australia, New Zealand, Cuba, Alaska, you name it! So now let us introduce our friend and a true **Guru of Real Estate Investing, *Ron LeGrand!***

Foreward
by Ron LeGrand

There are **3 main reasons** to read this book. The <u>first</u> is that it teaches **Creative Financing**, what I like to call **"Pretty House"** Strategies. This is where the **big money is,** and **the competition isn't.** When you learn the "Flip Side of Flipping" from this book, you'll definitely be taking the easier way to real estate riches.

I've never seen any other business where you can **control big-dollar assets** with a short phone call and one meeting, regularly **get huge checks** for tens of thousands in spendable cash, collect **passive cash flow** whether you work or not, and **build great wealth** over time with no effort.

These deals have the benefits of **no money down, no credit needed, no repairs, no holding costs, big and fast paydays, passive cash flow,** and **long-term appreciation.**

So do you <u>need</u> to learn this business? Only if you want to invest **7-10 hours** per week and make **$10,000** per month or much more. An average Pretty House deal has a profit of **$30,000**, so even if you only do one deal per month your yearly income will skyrocket.

This book is **the perfect place to start**, with its comprehensive and yet easy-to-understand explanations. It provides a great overview of how this business works, plus an amazing amount of <u>detail</u> and <u>specific instruction</u>.

<u>Second</u>, you want to **learn from the best**. The Wolff Couple are the **perfect trainers and authors** to teach you Creative Financing. (Of course I trained them, so you're really getting the best of the best).

I've taught Real Estate for over 35 years to over half a million students, and I will tell you **I have never met anyone like the Wolffs!**

When I met the Wolff Couple they already had **extensive experience** in real estate, including Lynette setting records as a New Home Sales Agent, and Brian managing an Ameriquest Mortgage office in downtown Phoenix. They soon created a thriving investing business in Arizona, where they've **become multi-millionaires** and closed over 700 house deals!

Now the Wolffs have been teaching on stage alongside me all across America for the last **15 years**. At our events they even collect the students' leads and **close Creative Financing deals *LIVE* on stage**. The students even get to keep all the profits! For many years they also taught my entire 4-day Pretty House Boot Camp, that's how much **trust and faith** I've always had in them.

<u>Third</u>, this book contains the actual **scripts, checklists, forms**, and **marketing samples** that the Wolffs' students use in their own businesses. These are the exact materials they put into action every day all across America *(and paid thousands for)*.

The Wolffs are **the industry experts** on scripts, marketing, selling fast, and "Acquisitionists". All these vital topics are covered here in this book.

Just like everything the Wolffs do, **this book far exceeds expectations**. It's like a **whole training course** right in your hands. These are the exact materials you need to get your business started.

I have **great respect** for the Wolffs professionally, and personally we've gotten to be **the closest of friends**. For over a decade we've **taken vacations together** all around the globe.

I count myself **very lucky** to have had these folks beside me, both on stage and in life, for so many blessed years *(with many more to come)!*

If you want my best advice, **get them on your side too!** You won't find any better teachers of real estate investing, or anybody who cares more about your personal success.

Even if you have no experience, if you have no cash and no credit, this book gives you a real chance to **close your 1st Creative Financing Deal!**

Buying this book may be the least expensive, most important thing you ever do!

Good Luck &
Good Investing,
Ron LeGrand

About the Authors, *The* **Wolff** *Couple*

The Wolff Couple have been training successful investors all across America for over **15 years**. Now **thousands of students** use their **proven investing materials** to create their futures through real estate investing.

Brian and Lynette are the **premier experts** on Scripts, *LIVE* Closing Calls, Pretty Houses, Acquisitionists, and Selling Homes Fast. They also work closely with renowned guru Ron LeGrand to provide amazing Live Training and Mentoring Programs. The Wolffs have taught so many of the current trainers in the field today that now students call them **"Mentors to the Mentors"**.

The Wolffs' backgrounds make them **uniquely qualified** to train you how to get rich in Real Estate. Lynette and Brian are straight talkers originally from Minnesota, with over **30 years** of experience. Lynette was a new home sales agent, and actually set an **Arizona state record** by selling **41** homes in one month! Brian was **Manager** of the downtown Phoenix Ameriquest Mortgage office, and a Realtor as well.

When the Wolffs truly focused on investing they quickly left those high paying jobs behind! Their investing business exploded, and continues to thrive with the help of their 2 sons, Dashel and Cale, and their other Acquisitionists and team. Even their daughter Trinity helps out!

The Wolffs **LOVE Pretty Houses!** You can make big profits when you just know **what to say**, every month you have huge **passive income**, and with an Acquisitionist the business is *done for you!*

Ron LeGrand knew the Wolffs were the **only ones for the job** when he hired them to teach his 4-day Pretty House Boot Camp. Not only were they **extremely successful investors**, Lynette was a master at selling Pretty Houses, and Brian's experience in negotiating mortgages made him ideally suited for Pretty House ("Terms") deals.

As an extra bonus, Brian had also **written screenplays in Hollywood** for 7 years, so he was perfect for creating all the powerful and conversational **scripts** needed to close Pretty House deals.

Since both Brian and Lynette previously managed offices, and have run their own for 15 years, they know **the key secrets of *Delegation*.** They are especially qualified to teach you how to hire, train, and manage your own Acquisitionist.

The day you make your first hire will be one of the **biggest steps up** in your entire investing career. One of the Wolffs' many nicknames is the **King & Queen of Automation and Delegation.**

The Wolff Couple have **trained so many of the top investors** out there, their **binder of testimonials** is thicker than a phone book. Brian and Lynette would love to help YOU truly **achieve your dreams** too!

The Wolffs look forward to talking with you by phone or seeing you at an upcoming event! **Please call** their office if you have any questions, or you see anything mentioned in this book you want to know more about. *It's very possible you'll get to speak to Brian and Lynette themselves!*

The Wolff Couple's Goal is <u>Your Success</u>!

"The Flip Side of Flipping"

Chapter 1
What is "The Flip Side of Flipping?"

When most folks think of Real Estate Investing, they think *"Flipping"!* The #1 Internet search term in the field is, of course, "Flipping". It seems like half the shows on certain TV networks have the work "Flipping" in the title. **People are flipping for *Flipping!* You must** be a bit curious about it yourself, or chances are you wouldn't be reading this book right now.

Why is Flipping so popular? Is it because half the populace are dying to dig into ugly houses and rip out toilets and go through all the headaches of renovating and reselling a trashed house? We think not. **It's what Flipping represents.** It's the imagined benefits of being a successful flipper. We're Brian and Lynette Wolff, and we imagined those benefits ourselves about 20 years ago. In upcoming pages we'll look closely at those **benefits of flipping**, and you'll see that some are real and some *are* actually imagined. We'll also take a close look at the only other well-known investing approach, the **"Buy & Hold" Strategy**, and consider its benefits and drawbacks as well.

Our evaluation of these two popular approaches, and our application of them in the real world, was not creating the results we were hoping and praying for. We knew we had to **discover a better way**…and we both had the same burning question.

Can we find a way of Real Estate Investing that offers all the best benefits, with none of the drawbacks?

It took us a long time to answer that question.

It took us a lot of research to answer that question. It took **Ron LeGrand** to answer that question.

Ron is the **renowned Real Estate Guru** who first exposed us to "The Flip Side of Flipping". We applied his training in the real world, started collecting huge checks, and **our lives changed forever**. Soon our personalities and backgrounds came into play, we refined everything we learned, and we **turned from students into teachers!**

Remember, we're not some flippers who made a few bucks and decided to cobble together some helpful tips into a book. <u>**This is our regular full-time job, training** and mentoring Real Estate Investors.</u>

We've taught real estate investing to hundreds of thousands of students all across North America for over 15 years. We show people how to make **a lot of money** in real estate, and honestly, we make good money doing it.

Yet right in these pages **we're revealing so much** of the training that our students have paid thousands of dollars for. Please don't underestimate **the power** of this material because you paid so little for it. This is the same precious money-making information our *Wolff Pack Members* get.

All we ask is that you study this material, then go **apply it in the real world** like we did, and our successful students do. If you follow what we teach you here, you can absolutely **make a huge income in your spare time.**

That's because we're going to **teach you a better way.**

It's a way that maybe 1 out 100 investors understands.

Would you like to learn a money-making model that conquers all the drawbacks of Flipping, and all the drawbacks of the Buy & Hold Strategy as well? Let's really **investigate those two popular approaches**, then we'll reveal the secrets of "The Flip Side of Flipping". We'll show you how ***Creative Financing* can change your life forever!**

As you move through this powerful book you'll see that we even included all the **scripts, checklists, forms**, and **marketing samples** you'll need to actually go out and **get your first deal**. How would you like a big check for $10,000, $20,000 or even more in the next month? How would that **change your life?**

Even more importantly, how would it change your life if you knew you could **systemize that process**, and keep cashing checks like that? What if you could quickly build a business that regularly receives those kinds of paydays? Plus you're not dealing with repairs, no nasty houses, no landlord troubles, **none of the drawbacks** typically associated with being a successful real estate investor.

Flipping has plenty of those headaches. The process itself is fairly simple – buy an ugly house, fix it up, and sell it for retail price to an owner occupant. We'll be going a lot more in-depth on that, but at its core it's that simple. Folks are not drawn to the "flipping process", they **desire what flipping represents**.

Most potential investors know there is some effort involved. It may be a simple process, but that doesn't mean it's easy. The effort is worth it though, because **Real Estate Investing represents an exciting new life in many ways:**

20 Benefits of Real Estate Investing

1. Huge Profits
2. Exciting Deal-making
3. Be Your Own Boss
4. Be the Director, Run the Show
5. Make Your Own Schedule
6. Enjoy Plenty of Time Off
7. Money Worries GONE
8. Lots Less Stress, Lots More Money
9. Happier Attitude
10. Work from Home
11. More Family Time
12. More Quality Time with Spouse/SO
13. Care for Extended Family
14. Donate to Church and Charities
15. Drive Your Dream Car
16. Live in Your Dream House
17. Take Dream Vacations
18. Enjoy Your Dream Life!
19. Do What You Want, When You Want

20. Freedom!

That's really what it comes down to, we want Freedom!

It's why we love America, land of the free. And you're never truly free as long as you're worrying about money, and working for someone else.

That's why people are drawn to flipping, and Real Estate Investing in general. Because it represents…

Freedom!

So what are the actual demands of "Flipping?" **Does Flipping really mean Freedom, or is that delusional?** And if flipping is hard, then who really wants to just **trade one rat race for another?**

Real Estate Investing should be an **Exit Strategy** to your current work. That means it shouldn't take that much time, or cause that much anxiety. So what's actually involved in the process of flipping, and is it **time-intensive and stressful?**

The 4 Steps to Flipping

1. Find Distressed House
2. Buy House
3. Fix House
4. Sell House for Profit

Find, Buy, Fix, Sell! 4 Easy Steps, right? **Not so fast.** A typical "Flip" is when an Investor finds an ugly house, buys it with cash or a mortgage loan (not Creative Financing), pays to repair it, then profits by selling to an owner occupant.

Because it's a **fairly intuitive process,** the general public can grasp it easily. That's why **most real estate Trainers stick to teaching flipping**. Also, very few investing Trainers actually comprehend the Creative Financing/*Flip Side* Strategies sufficiently enough to teach them.

So shows like **"This Old House" on PBS** started it all, and eventually **the flipping craze took over TV** (that **"Before & After" reveal** usually pays off big). Plenty of flipping books followed, and now there are lots of local Real Estate Investing Clubs that are jam-packed with? You guessed it, flippers and wannabe flippers.

So that's how the **general understanding of Real Estate Investing** turned to just one strategy, **"Flipping"**. But folks who have been around the industry for a while understand that Real Estate Investing **extends to many other strategies** and techniques.

While the **flipping model can be lucrative,** and is the most popularly understood version of Real Estate Investing, there are some really significant challenges to making it work for you.

Top **10** Challenges of **Flipping**

1. **Hard to** consistently **find** profitable deals on distressed houses – *lots of "newbie" flippers overpaying*

2. You might really dislike walking through ugly, dingy, **stinky houses** – *much nicer touring Pretty Houses!*

3. Must come up with **CASH to BUY** ugly houses, risk own hard-earned cash, or must locate and arrange Private Lender/friends/family for purchase money - *Banks won't loan on distressed properties*

4. Must come up with **CASH to REPAIR** house

5. Must have **CASH to cover HOLDING COSTS** (mortgage payments, taxes, insurance, HOA, etc.) during Renovations

6. Must work closely with **Contractors,** who because of the involved **process** and **personalities** can often be difficult, annoying, "misrepresenting", and woefully disorganized – *this can add tens of thousands of dollars and weeks or months of work to a Rehab.*

7. You end up doing some/much of the work **Yourself!** – *messes with your Time, Health, Relationships, and Overall Happiness*

8. Very common to **underestimate Repair Costs** and the **length of time** required, increasing Holding Costs - *entire profit may be lost*

9. The **Selling Process** can be **scary** and pressure-packed because you have **so much money and time** invested in the house, and you can ONLY sell to a qualified Cash-Out Buyer (no Lease Purchase Buyers) – *your Private Lender/family/friends may also be wanting constant updates, they want to know when they're getting their money back!*

10. If the house doesn't sell for cash immediately the whole scenario gradually **gets worse** in every way – *like a slow-motion car accident.*

Even with all these challenges, a lot of folks are out there chasing down "Flips"! That's because if you manage to **get it right**, you can make a heck of a **lot of money** in flipping.

Since our title is "The Flip Side of Flipping", let's **compare Flipping to Creative Financing deals** side by side. Remember on Flips you **pay cash** for ugly houses, rehab them, and then **sell through Realtors**. On Creative Financing deals you buy from "Pretty House" Sellers on **Terms**, then sell to **Lease Purchase Tenant Buyers**.

We'll be getting into the **important details** of how that works, for now let's just **evaluate the numbers**. We'll use a **market value of $200,000** for easy comparison.

	VS.	**Creative Finance**

Flip
Ugly House

VS.

Creative Finance
Pretty House

Market Value: **$200K**
Repairs: **- $30K**
Purchase Price: **- $130K**

CASH Buying Formula:
M.V. x 80% - Repairs = Maximum Allowable Offer **200K x 80% - 30K = 130K**

Big **challenge is finding** Ugly Houses you can buy at this **deep discount,** and finding them consistently (many are way overbid, some investors follow <u>no</u> formula).

Holding Costs: **- $5K**
Sales Costs: **- $15K Cash**
Sales Price: **+$200K**

Total Profit: <u>$20K</u>

Total Time: 2-6 months YOUR Time: *countless hrs* YOUR Hassles: *too many*

Huge challenge with this model is **no wealth-building passive income.** You stop rehabbing, you stop making money. This comparison also doesn't include when rehab costs run over, or when you get longer term or higher deposit on C.F. deals.

Market Value: **$200K**
Repairs: **- $2K**
Purchase Price: **- $190K**

You can afford to pay **top price** when you get other **favorable Terms.** Cosmetic **repairs** might be necessary.

Key is to get **TIME** from sellers to pay them off in full, usually 2-5 years, but often 10-30 yrs *(= wealth!)*

Length of Term: 5 years
Monthly Payment: $1200
Tenant-Buyer Rent: $1500
Cash Flow x 60 mo: **+$18K**
Non-Ref Deposit: **+$15K** *(Upfront Spendable Cash)*
Mortgage Paydown: **+$20K**
Holding Costs: **$0**
(Holding Time is 2-3 weeks)
Sales Costs:**- $2K** *(Stage BIG 1-Hr Open House)*

Terms Sales Price: **$220K** *(get 5-10% more on LP deals, plus Sales Price is in <u>5</u> years)* Back-End Profit: **+$15K** *(when Buyer gets new Mortgage)*

Total Profit: $64K

YOUR Time: *minimal* YOUR Hassles: *minimal (<u>not</u> Landlord, **they** do repairs)*

In this comparison we don't even include many of the **other profit sources** of Creative Financing deals. Those come from our **Main Exit Strategy: Lease Purchase Tenant Buyers**. The game-changing L.P. Program includes profit sources of Appreciation, Rent Increases, Depreciation, and more. Those factors can landslide the numbers thousands further **in favor of the "Flip Side"**.

So beyond the Creative Financing and Flipping models, is there any other legitimate and **well-known strategy** out there?

THE "BUY & HOLD" STRATEGY

The only other R.E.I. approach that has general public awareness is the **"Buy & Hold" Strategy**. Here the investor uses their **own cash and credit** to purchase a **limited number** of houses using institutional financing (banks). They try to buy at a good price, hold for years, and profit over time through positive cash flow, property appreciation, depreciation, and mortgage paydown.

This may sound okay…except that when you head down this path you have donned the mantle of *"Landlord"*. If you have never personally been a Landlord, it's hard to accurately convey the **daily aggravations** and occasion- ally **scary stretches** that dominate your existence. Plus it only seems to **get worse** as you get more properties.

Back when we were Landlording we had a little saying that somehow brought us solace. It was a recognition of our sorry state, and a required reinforcement of our diminished expectations. In those special moments of physical or emotional distress we would just mutter to each other, **"Headaches and backaches, that's what it takes."** Well guess what – *we was wrong!*

But before we found Creative Financing, we **paid plenty of dues** in the Buy & Hold world. Since this strategy is understood and practiced by many investors, it's important we review it more closely. You'll see how we **cherry-pick the best benefits** from the Buy & Hold strategy to structure powerful Creative Financing deals!

12 Challenges of the "Buy & Hold" Strategy

1. **Landlord** Headaches, Backaches, and Heartaches – *Tenants Create Big Time and Cash Demands*

2. Need **Good Credit** to Qualify for Financing, *and not too many other Mortgages on your Credit Report*

3. Need Large **Down Payment** to Close – *must find $*

4. Pay Substantial **Closing Costs** – *find more $*

5. **Repairs** and **Clean-Up** – *Costs Upfront Cash & Time*

6. Must Find and Work with **Dependable Contractor**(s) *to Complete Repairs within Time & Budget Goals*

7. Incur **Holding Costs** – *mtg payments, taxes, insurance, etc., while House is Repaired and Marketed*

8. **Small Deposit from Tenants** – *Not Even Close to Off-Setting Upfront Costs*

9. **Ongoing Repairs** and **Maintenance** – *Can Consume All Profits, Create Persistent Negative Cash Flow*

10. **Delinquencies** – *Add Major Stress, Take Time and Money to Resolve*

11. **Vacancies** – *Can Lose Yearly Profits in 1-2 Months*

12. **Banks Stop Extending Credit** – *Can't Buy More Houses, Business Is Frozen & Undercapitalized*

As you can see, the challenges of the **"Buy & Hold"** Strategy are financial, emotional, and considerable.

On this path you start by buying a house, usually through a Realtor off the Multiple Listing Service (the M.L.S. is an Internet service generally accessible only to licensed Agents). As a non-owner occupant you usually have to produce at least a 10% and probably a 20% **down payment.** Of course this is assuming you have good credit to start (which is a big assumption since many people don't), and that you're willing to **risk your credit.** Throw in **Closing Costs** on top of that, which can be many thousand dollars depending on your state.

Then the property often needs some **repairs or clean-up** to make it rentable for a good monthly amount. Even cosmetic fix-ups can run several thousand or more. Add the mortgage payments you have to make between the time you buy and the time you actually get it rented, and that's your **"Holding Costs".**

What does this add up to? On a $200,000 property you hope to invest UP FRONT as little at **$25,000,** but more probably it will come to over **$50,000! So where does all that money come from?** Probably your pocket.

I hate to pile on the poor "Buy & Holders", but even when you rent the house how much do the tenants give you up front? Just **a few grand,** first and last month's rent plus a damage deposit that they can get back. That doesn't put much of a dent in that huge wad of cash you already have into the house.

Depending on the financing, you hopefully set the deal up with $300+ **positive monthly cash flow.** This is the part we love! Cash flow on each house should bring in at least $3600 per year, up to as much as $12,000 or more.

We like to keep our estimates conservative, and for most properties you should realistically be hoping for around **$4000 - $5000 positive cash flow per year**. So good news, right?

Hold your horses. Sometimes this next challenge comes straight out of the blue, blowing up the entire model. What is this dark and foreboding menace to your profitability? The dreaded *Repairs and Maintenance!*

Let's say you have a house with a $4000 positive cash flow per year, an attractive Buy & Hold property. But then we get a hard rain and the roof needs some patching. Then the phone rings at 2:00 am because all the toilets are backing up and flooding the entire house. Then the air conditioning goes out on the hottest day of the year, and the repairman says you need a whole new unit. All of a sudden it's like, **where did all those profits go?**

On top of all that, we hate to break it to you, but what if one of your tenants run into a rough patch? It's your favorite tenant, and you've got nothing but excuses from them for the last 45 days. Then another tenant moves out without paying and leaves a mess behind. After the clean- up you're having challenges moving it, prospective renters keep flaking out on showings, and now you've been **sitting on a vacancy** for 30-60+ days.

Let's face it, as a Landlord you're **living a precarious existence**. You're surviving on some **skinny margins**, and saying your prayers at night that all your A/C units last through the summer.

Even if all that doesn't dissuade you, and you still want to **build a Buy & Hold empire**, there's one last massive roadblock. Once you have a certain number of mortgage loans on your personal credit report, or a certain level of debt (regardless of the off-setting income), **banks will start saying "No"**!

When the mortgage loans dry up, the business is suddenly **under-capitalized** and **stagnated**. At this point *Buy & Hold becomes Sit & Wait!* You might pick up a property when you can get scrape together extra cash, but it's probably a long time between additions to the portfolio (you'll see that this is **not an issue** on "the Flip Side", where nothing but you holds you back).

Yet all these Buy & Hold challenges would be worth it, all the headaches and heartaches, for that sweet **Long- Term Profit**. You'd gladly trade your toil if you could follow this path to a gradual **amassing of wealth**. Now hold onto that thought, because we are about to show you exactly how to do that *the better way.*

The Buy & Hold Strategy contains **3 Key Factors** to <u>**Wealth Accumulation**</u> – 1) Holding high-dollar assets **growing in value** 2) Assets being **paid off with O.P.M.**, *Other People's Money* 3) Assets producing substantial **monthly income**. Those aspects of the model are **very exciting**, there is **HUGE long-term profit** in the "Buy & Hold" Strategy… if we could just avoid the drawbacks.

That is eminently possible. In fact, we have students who **own a massive number of homes** which they bought with **little or no money down**. Many of them are reformed flippers, and now they're buying properties correctly. The house mortgages don't even show up on their credit reports, plus they earn **huge positive cash flow**.

Here's one of our students who's an awesome example:

Andrew Schlag - *Evansville, IN*

 Since I started with the Wolffs' systems I have bought over **200** homes, and gained well over **2 million $$$** in cash and equity! I still own a lot of the homes, and I make over **$10,000** per month in **Passive Income!** My brother now works with me as a partner as well as 2 FT Assistants.

We just finished another deal, bought it "Subject to" for $102,000, sold it for $142,000 with $5000 down payment. Plus the debt pay-down in the meantime.

They just cashed us out after 5 months!!! This deal just made us a **$40,000** profit, that's $8000 per month on only 1 deal. We also make thousands per month in **Passive Income cash flow**  on houses we used to flip for just one paycheck.

 Thank you to the Wolff Couple, and I thank the Lord for this awesome opportunity. I also thank my Dad, mom and brother for being such big supporters and help in this endeavor. Thank you thank you thank you, you ALL are awesome!!!!! I thank the Lord and the Wolff Couple!!!

This is awesome!
- *Andrew Schlag*

P.S. The Wolffs wanted me to tell you I'm only 25 years old!

Let's look at some **potential numbers**. Say you owned **50 houses**, and you owed exactly what they were worth, but none of the debt was in your name. You may have no equity, but the houses average **$300 positive cash flow** each. That's **$15,000 profit** every month! That's just one component of the formula for creating **great wealth**, even *intergenerational* wealth. You use other people's money to control valuable assets that pay you a big cash flow.

Would $15,000 per month cover your living expenses?

The thing is, by pursuing the Buy & Hold Strategy you will never get to 50 houses. Buying properties the smarter way you can own 50 houses, **you can own 100 houses**, and no bank can say "No" to you. Plus when you follow the right way we laid out here, it won't take you that long.

Remember we're just talking about the monthly cash flow here. We're not taking into account any of the other **major profit sources of Creative Financing**, some of which are the same as "Buy & Hold" (appreciation, depreciation, and mortgage balance paydown).

The **down and dirty truth** of the "Buy & Hold" Strategy is that you **need cash and credit** to make it work. It's usually a lot of **your own money** at the start, plus some pricey bank money or "hard" money. You are putting your **credit at risk**, which we never want you to do (and you never have to do). The whole point of investing smarter is doing it with **very little to no risk**.

You can really only hope to get in the Buy & Hold game if you've got a pretty **hefty entry fee**, plus **good credit**. Those 2 requirements are the **primary barriers** (and potential game-enders) to most hopeful new investors. They don't have the down payments, nor the capital (financial cushion) they need to weather the market, and get through their own learning curve.

We have the solution to no money and no credit, and **all the challenges** presented by the Flipping and Buy & Hold Models. Even if you have money and credit, why take chances when you can **do deals without risk?**

So what is the way we discovered, that Ron LeGrand first revealed to us, that has turned out to be **the true path** for us and thousands of students? What type of lucrative real estate deals are <u>not</u> found on any TV Shows? **What is the "Flip Side of Flipping"?**

CREATIVE FINANCING!

These Strategies are commonly known by several different names — *Terms Deals, Pretty House Deals, Owner Financing, Seller Carryback, Seller Mortgage, Sandwich Lease Purchases, etc.* These Strategies are defined by the fact that **we don't use our own money or credit.** Now that requires a little creativity sometimes, that's where the Creative Financing part comes in.

You may have heard about some of these methods. They've been around as long as land ownership and the barter concept. The clever folks in each time period are the ones who *secured the most land for the least amount of their own money and credit.* **That's the exact goal of Creative Financing**, to own and/or control the most assets for the least amount of money. **That's the game.**

Creative Financing simply works better than any other Investing Strategy. It gives you the most freedom and flexibility, with both your money and your time.

How much cash do you want to give the seller upfront?
Little or Nothing Down.

Do you want to use and risk your own credit to finance it?

No Credit.

Other methods require cash, or credit, or both! Other strategies require repairs, time to do them, time to sell the house, and cash to cover the holding costs in the meantime. Creative Financing requires none of those things. Here's a great example, a 1st deal from students who now make hundreds of thousands per year.

Alicia & Todd Foster - *Burnsville, MN*

So we have our first Creative Financing deal officially closed!!! We got a deposit check for $12,000 (spendable cash) and another for $1,500 (1st month's rent). The total non-refundable option deposit was **$15,000!**

It was a **NO MONEY DOWN / NO CREDIT NEEDED Deal, just like you taught us!**

We spun our wheels in real estate for a while before meeting you two. Your training is quite honestly the coolest thing ever invented. Knowing "What to Say" and "What to Do" like you teach **made our lives so much easier and gave us so much more confidence!**

We are embarrassed to admit how many Investing systems we purchased in the last couple years. There are none like yours, it was exactly what we were searching for and needed to get us going. Our total profit will be a little over **$47,600!!!!** We just wanted to say THANK YOU, THANK YOU, THANK YOU!

We love the Wolff Couple!
Hoooowwl!

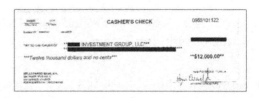

Creative Financing is simply **the smartest way** to structure deals so you pay little or nothing down, and use other people's money and credit for financing.

That's how it works on the ***BUYING SIDE!***
Then comes the ***SELLING SIDE!***

How you sell a property is called your "**Exit Strategy**". That is a **major key** to why the Creative Financing model works so well. Over 95% of the time your Exit Strategy will be selling to a **"Lease Purchase Tenant Buyer"**.

Here's how to recognize and target market for them.

Lease Purchase Tenant Buyer

- Currently **Unable to Qualify** for a Bank Mortgage Due to 1 or More Factors *(ads say "Bad Credit OK")* -- rough credit, too much debt, self-employed, not reporting all income hurts debt ratio, new to area, short time on job, etc.

- **Credit Repair** or other Assistance will eventually enable Buyer to Qualify

- Has at least **$10,000** or **5%** of the Purchase Price for a **Non-Refundable Option Deposit**, which will be applied towards the **Down Payment** & **Purchase Price** of Home when Buyer Qualifies for new Bank Financing -- Ask *"What's the most you can put down on your beautiful new home?" (Get most you can)*

- Can Afford **Monthly Payment** *("Most u can pay/mo?")*

- Will Pay a **5%-10% Mark-Up** on Purchase Price in Exchange for the **Opportunity** for Financing Help

There are a dozen reasons why this works so well.

12 Lease-Purchase Program Paydays

1. **Non-Refundable Option Deposit** = *Big Instant Profit It's common to get at least 5%, and often closer to 10% of the Purchase Price from your Tenant Buyer* **upfront***. This is* **spendable CASH** *to you, and converts to* **Down Payment** *when they qualify.*

2. Get **5-10%+ Higher Purchase Price** due to Financing *When you accept Buyers with Bad Credit or other qualifying issues they rarely question the price.*

3. Seller makes 1-3 more Monthly Mortgage Payments

4. **Positive Monthly Cash Flow** from Rent
   Aim for $300 - $500+ per month per home

5. Tenant Buyers **pay for repairs**, upkeep, improvements ***HUGE KEY*** *to why this works, and why you are not stuck being a Landlord!*

6. **Mortgage Balance Reduction**
   Massive Income Source over time, **$10,000+/Deal**

7. **Depreciation** -- *Write off profits for yearly tax savings*

8. **Appreciation** -- *Property Values go up*

9. Mortgage Interest **Tax Deduction** -- *More write-offs*

10. If Tenant Buyer moves, get **Another Option Deposit**

11. Get back **Escrow Account Funds** when Cashing Out

12. **Discount Seller Financing** at Cash-Out Closing
    We call this "the deal after the deal" = more profit!

Now you may think **you need some training** to understand some of those paydays, and you'd be right. **Creative Financing** and **Lease Purchases** are not quite so simple as <u>Find</u>, <u>Buy</u>, <u>Fix</u>, <u>Sell</u>, remember? In fact, maybe you're not even sure what some of these terms mean exactly. Well no worries, **that's why we wrote this book.** So the **smart folks like you who read it will have a massive advantage** over 99% of the other investors out there. Because we're revealing to you that...

CREATIVE FINANCING IS WHERE THE MONEY IS.

Pretty Houses abound. In most areas over 90% of the houses for sale are Pretty, and those are our target for Creative Financing Deals. This **opens up vistas** for you "traditional" investors, now you can call on any house for sale, not just "junkers". Other investors are busily **chasing those ugly houses** anyway, **driving the prices too high.**

The real beauty of Creative Financing is the **avoidance of the dangers and traps** of Real Estate Investing. **There is NO RISK when you're not risking anything.** In these deals you never use your own credit, so it's never at risk. You use no cash or only small amounts, only when absolutely necessary, and it's returned shortly (plus much more) when your Lease Purchase Tenant Buyer gives you their "**Non-Refundable Option Deposit**".

This is a **great time** for you if you're just getting into this, because **Technology** has absolutely changed the face of this business. Everything is exponentially easier now. Cell phones have their challenges, but they make it so much easier to reach Sellers and Buyers. **Texting** is a **major component** of that ease of access, and you'll use it constantly.

The Internet has also revolutionized Real Estate Investing. At your fingertips is so much information about individual properties, "farm areas", companies, lenders, other investors, or customers. **Zillow.com**

is replete with vital information. It's a **powerful resource** for finding and evaluating properties, as well as being a far-reaching marketing tool. You'll need to get familiar with and use Zillow regularly to **locate, research,** and **pre-screen** prospects, as well as **post your own properties for sale.**

With the investing world growing, TV exposure broadening, and real estate websites constantly evolving, how is it possible you've never heard that much about **Creative Financing?** With the popularity of flipping, why isn't the **better *Flip Side* way** more on your radar?

Why haven't these Creative Financing Strategies become popular the way "Flipping" has? Well, it's complicated. I don't mean the answer is complicated, I'm saying Creative Financing can be complicated. That's why you don't see a bunch of shows about Creative Financing. They stick to flipping because it's easy to explain – Find, Buy, Fix, Sell. Plus you get that one emotional *"Before & After"* **reveal shot** per episode.

Creative Financing might be a little complicated, but **we're here to make it easy for YOU!** We've gone way beyond understanding these strategies and techniques, **we've lived them and taught them for 15 years**. We've profited greatly from them, we've structured them into **simple systems**, and we've done all we can to pass them on to our student-investors.

These Creative Financing Strategies are so **extremely lucrative,** and when you follow our systems it won't take you long before you're structuring deals like our students from Texas here, Cammy and Kyle.

Kyle & Camille - *Humble, TX*

We thank you again for your ongoing education, and the motivation to Take Action and "get things done!" We closed on yet another owner finance deal and wanted to share the results.

We purchased the property for $91,000, then sold it "as is" for a price of $116,000. We received a $25,000 down payment and financed $91,000 at 9% for 20 years. With this "sweetheart" financing we may make over $100K by the time the deal is done! The new owners are first time homebuyers and are so excited to have their first home.

We did another deal where just the profit from the rent will total $17,096 over the first 3 years, with an eventual grand total of $103,775.

This will really help toward retirement. That one deal included the following methods: Subject To, Lease Purchase, Work for Equity, Owner Finance, and a Wrap-Around Mortgage. We are so thankful for all you have taught us, <u>we never could've done this without you</u>!

You're reading the book, now it's

Time to Take Action!

Call Our Office Now or Go to the
Website Below to Order Our Amazing

"Pretty House Power Pack"
(Retail Price $497) ONLY $97!

(with CODE below)

Entire Manual on Pretty House Deals
Online Videos/Audios OR DVD & CD
- All the Tools You Need

Start Closing Creative Financing Deals TODAY!
Make Huge Option Deposits FAST, Earn Passive Monthly
Cash Flow, Build Long-Term Wealth!

CALL 888-Rich-Now

(1-888-742-4669)
OR go to PrettyHousePower.com
Save $400 w/ **Coupon Code FSF400PHPP**

Limited Number of Systems Available
ACT NOW So You Don't Miss Out!

Duffy Ford - *Louisville, KY*

I wanted to tell you how excited I am! I cannot wait to implement more of the systems I learned from you to take my business to the next level.

Since meeting you guys just 12 months ago we've **purchased 2 properties subject to, and 3 foreclosures. The total profits from these deals should net us over $275,000!!!**

As exciting as that sounds, I am even more thrilled and motivated to implement the new lessons learned in marketing, talking to sellers, talking to buyers, the 1-Hour Home Sale, and hiring an Acquisitionist. Those will quickly catapult my business to the 7-figure level!

Why is it sometimes **challenging for the average person**, even the average investor, to **grasp the concepts** of Creative Financing? First of all, Flipping is relatively intuitive, and easily understandable.

In many cases the opposite is true for **Creative Financing**, it can be **counter-intuitive**. How can you buy a house, pay full price, and still make a quick $20,000 or more? Maybe it doesn't make sense to you right now, yet it happens to our students all the time!

Check out this next student deal example where that's exactly what happened.

Dan Kapornyai - *Richmond, VA*

Take a look at this check! We are so excited to have the home sold! Thank you so much. Learning to sell a house has been a struggle for

me, but then you taught me to get the buyers there and create a sense of urgency. That's exactly what I did. The buyers told me to go ahead and said take the signs down, we want the house!

We made $15,000 on the front end, $250 positive monthly cash flow and we'll make about $14,000 on the back end. That's about a $30,000 profit with a 2-year Lease Purchase agreement after buying "Subject to" from the seller. Thanks so much, we're really looking forward to our next deal!

Janna - *Plano, TX*

I just want to say thanks to y'all! Several years ago we found ourselves **in debt for the first time** due to **2 major surgeries** in one year. This began a roller coaster of debt for us. My son Toby had large student loan debt. So this was a **BIG DEAL!**

I decided to send a yellow letter to a property I knew about, and she called me within a few days. We met at the property. Repairs needed were about $75K. The owner had passed on 2 years ago.

The owner was the ex-wife that was left on the deed, she **did not want the property** at all. The taxes were behind almost $20K, this property was a huge burden to her. I remembered what you said. "The first person who mentions price loses!" So I asked "What is the least you'll take?" She said, **$100K. I said, "DONE!"** I didn't even ask her if that was the best she could do like you teach us to do! My husband had to walk away just to compose himself!

We purchased it quickly. The seller told me she had a stack of investor letters about 6 inches tall. After receiving my yellow letter, she called ME! I WAS SOOO THANKFUL! After talking to Lynette, she advised that we sell quickly. I am so thankful we **did not rehab – what a headache!!** I did what she said and I contacted all of the investors. We sold it a few weeks later for $230,000 — "as is" plus they pay all closing costs. Our CHECK from the Title Agent was **$103,233.62!!!**

Last Friday on August 12, 2016, we sat down and **paid off ALL of our personal debt,** my son's student loans, around $64,000 of debt. We are **DEBT FREE** for the first time in years!!! **We are so grateful to the Lord for His provision and for y'all!**

I am just a simple **stay-at-home mom**! My giftedness is speaking and teaching, NOT business! I have to go over and over this stuff to get it! AND I am a horrible time manager! I love to play! If I can do this, **ANYBODY CAN DO THIS!!!**

Thank you Brian and Lynette for giving to us your teaching and encouragement! We appreciate you so much!

May God Bless you as you help others like me and my family!!!

Some deals make intuitive sense, but what if you heard of a deal where you could **pay more than the house is worth** and still **profit over $20,000**? That type of Creative Financing Deal is called a "Long-Term Lease Purchase", or an "Assigning Contract Terms" Deal. Deal structuring like that is unheard of, unless you know us and Ron LeGrand. On its face **it doesn't seem to make sense!** It will all become clearer as you progress through this book, and start reading over the scripts explaining it to Prospects. You'll soon see that these deals do **make massive dollars and ~~cents~~ sense!**

THE "ADDING VALUE" CONUNDRUM

The reason some Creative Financing deals don't seem to make sense, is that investors can't see **_why_** they are making money on it. How are they "**Adding Value**"? Flipping doesn't require contemplation on that, you're adding value through repairs and upgrades. But if you buy a Pretty House that needs no repairs for near retail price, how is there **any spread** in that?

The answer lies in the **"time value of money"**. _You get time from the Seller by working with the existing mortgage or other seller financing, then you give your Tenant Buyer some of that time to get qualified, and they pay a premium for that opportunity._ Do you understand that single sentence? **Read it over 3 times,** because that's the essence of the Creative Financing business.

You don't add value by renovating, you add it through **smart Deal Structuring**. First you get the Seller's agreement by explaining the deal correctly on the phone (using **_Scripts_**). Your added value comes from persuading the Seller to agree to favorable **"Terms"**. Then you turn around and provide that Pretty House on **slightly higher terms** to a Tenant Buyer. The added value for your Tenant Buyer lies in the chance to live in a beautiful home, and have time to resolve their credit or other qualifying issues in order to own it. It is **a wonderful thing** telling folks they get to live in these gorgeous homes, especially couples with young families. There have been times with plenty of **tears of joy** all around!

Your Tenant Buyers might devote themselves to repairing their qualifying issues and getting their new mortgage, but it doesn't always go that way (and that's **a good thing**). Often Buyers experience some unexpected turn of events that results in them moving out. Then you KEEP their BIG DEPOSIT, plus you get the house back to collect **another Deposit!** You can make **tens of thousands** just on this one L.P. income stream.

In other cases (and depending on how much you push it), your **Tenant Buyers** will get their credit repaired, gather their down payment, and **line up a new mortgage**. This generally takes anywhere from around 12 months to many years. When you have good positive cash flow (Passive Income), your policy will become the same as ours -- *"Set it and forget it."*

In almost every case, **the longer you hold onto a property the more money you make**. When you get a long term from your Seller, you DO NOT want to push your Buyer to cash you out. You'd rather have **many years of profits** from positive monthly cash flow, property appreciation, depreciation, mortgage balance paydown, tax advantages, and more.

We've seen countless thousands of fresh-faced Investors since we started training folks in 2003. Many of them **didn't have the money or credit** to buy houses through bank loans, so they had no choice but to **start with Creative Financing**. Maybe you're in that same boat. Don't fret – **this book is all about deals that don't take any cash or credit!** The fact that this book is in your hands right now is either destiny, good fortune, or an **answer to prayers** (we like to think all three)!

Is Investing "Sales"...and Can I Sell?

You might not have the most positive reaction when you hear people talk of Real Estate Investing being a "Sales" field. Even the word *Sales* might make you a little anxious. We've taught Real Estate Investing to tens of thousands of students for over 15 years, and we never call it "Sales Training". We're going to let you in on **a little secret** – *some of it is Sales Training!*

Calm your concerns now, there's nothing to be anxious about! My (Brian's) grandma would always say, **"You can fret, but then that's all you get."** You want more than a pile of anxieties, you want a **pile of cash!** After all, what really are the "Sales" aspects of Real Estate Investing, and should they make you anxious? It's just **being friendly** on the phone, reading through some **proven scripts**, then meeting to get a **little paperwork** done.

Let's dig deeper by reviewing this list. As you can see, none of these Action Steps below should be overly daunting, many of them have nothing to do with sales, and the others only require **a little training to be effective**. That "Sales" training includes reading over the scripts, practicing them, and all- important **Role-Playing** (use the amazing Role-Play DVDs and Flashcards in our Wolff-LeGrand **"What to Say"** Script System).

12 Basic Action Steps to Buy a House

1. Prescreen Seller Lead
2. Choose Matching "Closing Call" Script
3. Dial Phone - *not as simple as it sounds*
4. Be Friendly to Seller - *take time on good leads*
5. Read Proven Script into Phone - *explain deal*
6. Answer Questions or Objections - *using Scripts*
7. Set Appointment - *for "Deal Meeting"*

8. Type and Print Agreement – *call our office to get*
9. Meet Seller - *usually at property*
10. Tour House - *take pictures, notes*
11. Work Out Any Last Deal Points
12. Show Seller Where to Sign

Some of these Action Steps are administrative or executive, others could technically be considered Sales, but we don't label them that. Harness the power of **"Transformational Vocabulary"** whenever you can, by **using words that empower you & give you confidence**.

You're just "being friendly on the phone", and "following proven scripts". That's all Sales is anyway, being nice, reading scripts, and then **asking for a "Yes"**.

3 Steps of the Sales Process

1. Make Friends – *Build Rapport*
2. Present the Benefits – *Why They Should Say "Yes"*
3. Ask for the Sale – *an Appointment or a Signature*

That doesn't seem all that hard, does it? Yet we still get a little anxious about "Sales", and certainly part of that is the **fear of rejection**. Just remember **this one truth – they NEVER reject you.** That's right, you never get rejected in this business.

You offer Sellers a certain plan, which involves them giving you **a little time to pay them off in full**. The Sellers have their own plan, and if theirs doesn't fit with yours, they will **REJECT your PLAN**. It'll be a "No", and there's not much you can do about it.

But they are **not rejecting you personally**. Sometimes it feels kind of personal, especially the way some suspects say "No". Just remember they are never rejecting you, they are rejecting your plan for buying their house. Here's a favorite saying we have in our office, *"Even if they* **make** *it personal, don't* **take** *it personal."*

Now if that was your one and only lead, then it is obviously more distressing. You just have to **get more leads**, and use the proven scripts on more Sellers. The very next one might say **"Yes"** with a big smile and an attitude of gratitude.

If the Sellers don't have a set plan, or their plan is **flexible** enough to give you time and take little or nothing down, then you're in business! You'll be able to help that prospect!

Let us make one more important point. Other Investors may be anxious about the Creative Financing Business because **they have to talk to prospects**. They only want to submit low bids on junkers on their computer or through an agent, and anything else scares them off. That's a good thing, because it **weeds out the competition**. You're not like that, **you're tough!**

You know the steps to take, and "Sales" doesn't make you flinch. To answer the question posed in the title of this section, **"YES, you can sell!"**

With us and Ron LeGrand you have the training, the proven scripts, and the confidence you need to succeed! If you need more motivated seller leads, or any other help with Scripts or Systems, you know we have the resources to help.

Just call our office at 888-Rich-Now, talk to our staff, and we'll do our best to set up a time when we can **talk with you one-on-one personally.**

5 MUSTS

for Starting Your Own Creative Financing Investing Business

1. You MUST hear about **Creative Financing** from some website or person, preferably a trusted source *(Us and Ron LeGrand)*

2. You MUST think **"outside-the-box"** enough to **recognize the wealth-making opportunity.**

3. You MUST **believe in yourself and your skills** enough to think you can succeed at this.

4. You MUST **decide to pursue** Pretty House Profits!

5. You MUST **get Trained** so you know what you're doing, and can close complicated deals effectively.

Fortunately **you now have The Wolff Couple** on your side. Now **5) getting Trained** is solved! We are the best Trainers and wingmen for success in the entire country. You should see all the Creative Financing Deals that we **close for our students** when we travel to their cities on our **2-Day Field Trips!**

We recently **flew to New Mexico** to work alongside four of our students who had teamed up. We had **14** appointments, wrote **10** contracts, and generated deals with over a **$300,000 Profit potential in less than 48 Hours!** On one particular luxury home alone the Sellers signed over to us over **$200,000 of Free Equity**!

Bill, Jennifer, Michele, JoAnn – *New Mexico*

It's amazing to see how these Creative Financing techniques work up close. I'm not exaggerating when I say this really turned a corner for us. In fact, after the Wolffs left town we went out and closed 2 more deals on our own The Sellers signed the agreement on our very first visit We had never done that before, but when you see what's really possible nothing can hold you back We're looking at a positive cash flow of over $3500 and option deposits of over $100K Thank you so much for showing us the real way to do real estate investing.

1.

Okay, I'm going to tell a little tale now on Bill and Jennifer. They had gotten hundreds of leads, and somehow they **couldn't get one closed**. Then we came to town and showed them how, and now they're **off to the races!** You can be just like them (the successful part)!

Just apply what we're teaching in this book, get one deal done, and your life will never be the same! You will understand and own a special segment of your market.

Other Investors Are Too Scared or Ignorant
to Pursue Creative Financing Deals,
So You Have Way Less Competition!

I don't mean "ignorant" as a judgmental or pejorative term, although it tends to carry that weight. Ignorant doesn't mean stupid, it just means **uninformed** and **untrained**. I'll put it that way too, since you may personally have been one of those "ignorant" Investors before picking up this game-changing book.

OTHER INVESTORS ARE TOO SCARED OR UNTRAINED, SO YOU HAVE WAY LESS COMPETITION!

Thank goodness **you found the best training** anywhere when you found us. It started, no question, with the master, **Ron LeGrand**. Then we took everything we ever learned from Ron, added all our own experience and insights, and then **systemized it** for others.

Now don't think that your Real Estate Training will start and end with this short book. **This is just the beginning.** Real Estate Investing is a multi-million dollar, often complicated industry.

Therefore we have created **in-depth home training courses** on all the specialized areas we cover in this book. That includes Marketing for Sellers, What to Say to Sellers & Buyers (Scripts), What to Do (Systems), Getting Rich with Realtors, The 1-Hour Home Sale (Open House Training), profiting with an Acquisitionist, and so much more! We even have a powerful system for getting the right Mindset called "Psych Ups" *(866-Psych-Up)!*

Call our office at **888-Rich-Now** and we'll help you with any questions or anything you need. **We've been where you are, so we know what you need!**

Now let's go really **in-depth** and get some true detail on the **Flipping deal** and the **Creative Financing deal**, to see where they compare and contrast.

<u>Flipping Step-by-Step Checklist</u>
<u>Ugly House Seller + Cash-Out Buyer</u>

1. Set up a work space, and schedule 5-10 hours/week to be there making calls, marketing, etc.
2. Plan how to take incoming calls, set up phone/answering service/Assistant.
3. Make Outbound Seller Calls to *"FSBOs"* and *"For Rents"* (scripts on Wolffs' Forms CD).
4. Pick 4+ ways to Market for Sellers & Buyers. Get necessary Marketing forms with ad copy.
5. Order business cards and signs, or make signs. Place Internet / Craig's List / Classified Ads.
6. If available, find a source for Pre-foreclosure houses (M.L.S., gov't, pay websites, etc.).
7. Print letters/flyers, esp. Pre-foreclosure/Foreclosure flyers/letters. Get letters/flyers out.
8. Keep distributing all marketing materials, passing out business cards, and getting ads out.

9. Find listed Ugly Houses / Foreclosures / Short Sales. Call Listing Realtors, make aggressive offers. Have those Realtors find more Ugly Houses / Foreclosures / Short Sales for you to make offers on. Repeat until several Realtors are working with you.

10. Locate "Ants"/Bird Dogs/ Field Agents to drive for Dollars and take pics. Get them sending leads.

Ongoing Action Steps

1. Take calls from sellers/buyers, fill out intake forms. Prescreen out suspects, keep prospects. Use *Opening Call* notes.

2. Get info on prescreened property from Internet (Zillow, County Recorder and/or Tax Assessor, etc.).

3. Pull "Comps" for prescreened property off Internet, RealEstateABC.com, MLS, or from Realtor contact.

4. Go see property (or Assistant see it). Take pics.

5. List all necessary repairs and clean-ups. Estimate Costs -- $5000, $10,000, $15,000, etc.

6. Call back prescreened seller prospects. Read *Closing Call* Script (**Ugly House Seller**). Answer questions and objections, then read *Setting the Appointment*

7. **OR** submit offer through Realtor.

8. (if no Realtor) Go on appointment, sign purchase contract with seller.

9. Send contract to title company or attorney to get title report. If they find any title issue have them help clear it up. Make sure you can get clear title before you proceed.

10. Order repair estimates from painter/flooring guy/other contractors.

11. Order all necessary repairs & clean-up to be done.

12. Set up insurance and take over utilities on property (and H.O.A. if applicable).

13. Schedule, then supervise progress of repair work.

14. After repair and clean up work is completed, "stage" the house with pictures/plants/etc. Put a lock box on the front door containing a key so buyers can view home easily.

15. Call any prospects on Cash-Out Buyers List. Read *Closing Call* Script (**Cash Out Buyers**).
16. Post "For Sale, All New Inside" signs in yard and on corners around house.
17. Print up flyers. Leave flyers & applications in house.
18. Take new pictures for marketing, get on flyers and your website with enthusiastic ad.
19. **NOTE:** You can also choose to list house with a Realtor. Make sure there's enough net profit to afford commission. You can always negotiate a lower commission, or consider paying a higher percentage commission for a quicker sale on a graduated scale.
20. Place ads for property on Internet, Zillow, Craigslist, Classified Ads under "Houses for Sale"
21. Take **Opening Calls** from Cash-Out Buyer prospects, fill out "**Pretty House Buyer Call Script**". Prescreen by how well qualified they are, and how quickly they can close.
22. Follow up with prescreened Cash-Out Buyers. Read *Closing Call* Script (**Cash Out Buyer**). Answer any questions and objections, then set appointment to close.
23. Meet with Cash-Out Buyer to get **Purchase Agreement** signed **OR** work through Realtor.
24. Schedule closing with buyer and your attorney. Attorney should handle all details.
25. Move pictures/plants/etc. (staging kit) out of property.
26. After Cash-Out Buyer moves in, deliver gift basket, ask for referrals (offer referral gift/bonus).

Creative Financing Step-by-Step Checklist
Pretty House Seller + Lease Purchase Buyer

by *The* **Wolff** *Couple*.com

1. Set up a work space, and schedule **5-10 hours/week** to be there making Calls, Marketing, etc.
2. Get Business **Phone** Line. Plan how to take incoming calls, set up Answering Service/Assistant.
3. Pick 4+ ways to **Market** for Sellers. Get necessary Marketing forms with ad copy *(samples here)*.
4. Order **Business Cards** and **Signs**, or make Signs.
5. Place Internet / Craigslist / Classified **Ads**.
6. Make **Outbound Calls** to *"FSBO"* Sellers and Landlords under *"Houses For Rent"*.
7. Get letters / flyers / doorhangers printed. Mail letters, get flyers / doorhangers distributed.
8. Keep distributing all **Marketing Materials**, passing out Business Cards, and getting ads out.

Ongoing Action Steps

1. **Take Calls** from sellers/buyers, fill out intake forms. Prescreen out suspects, keep prospects.
2. Get info on prescreened property from Internet (**Zillow.com, County Recorder, etc.**).
3. Pull **"Comps"** for prescreened property off Internet, **RealEstateABC.com**, MLS, or Realtor contact.
4. Call back prescreened seller prospects, read matching **Closing Call Script** (Pretty House Seller)
5. Answer any questions or **Objections**, then read the **"Setting the Appointment" Script**.
6. Go on Appointment. **Tour House. Take Notes** on "Features & Fixes". **Take Pics** for Marketing.
7. Go through **Deal Meeting Script** w/ Seller. Sign initial agreements. Help them turn over Zillow Listing.
8. Get all of seller's **paperwork** on the house and any mortgages

(see Seller Congrats Letter).

9. Send contract to title company or attorney to get **Title Report**. If they find any title issue have them help clear it up. Make sure you can get **clear title** before you proceed.

10. Schedule **closing appointment** for seller and your real estate **attorney**. Ask seller if you can **show house** before then (if looks nice)

11. Give list of any repairs/clean up to seller. See if they'll fix up a few things before showings.

12. Order **repair estimates** from contractor/painter/flooring person/handyman/etc.

13. After seller moves out, Order necessary **repairs** and **clean-up** work to be done before showings.

14. After repairs and clean up, **"Stage"** the house with pictures/plants/plug-in aromatics, etc. Put a **lock box** on the front door containing a key so buyers can view home easily.

15. Take **new pics** for flyers and website if the house looks much better (often use prior **Zillow** pics).

16. Put property pics and an enthusiastic description on Zillow.com and your selling website.

17. **Place ads** for property on Internet/Craig's List/Classified Ads/etc. ("Bad Credit OK!")

18. Post "For Sale, Rent-to-Own" **Signs** in yard, and on corners around house.

19. Print up flyers/doorhangers. Leave marketing Flyers and lease purchase **Applications** on counter.

20. Market for the **"1-Hour Open House"**. Follow procedure on **Step #22** for incoming callers.

21. Call prescreened prospects on **Lease Purchase Tenant Buyer's List**. Read **Closing Call** Script (Lease Purchase Buyer Section). Answer any questions or objections, Set Appt for showing.

22. **Schedule Private Showings** for Buyers with $10K-$20K+. Schedule rest to come to Open House.

23. Take **Opening Calls** from Tenant Buyer prospects, fill out

"Pretty House Buyer Info Script". Prescreen mostly by Option Deposit amount, also Monthly Payment, then follow *Step #22*.

24. Follow up with prescreened Tenant Buyers. Read Lease Purchase Buyer *Closing Call* Script. Answer any questions or Objections, then set Appointment to close.

25. Prepare, Stage, and Hold a **"1-Hour Open House"**. See our "1-Hour Home Sale" System for all the necessary Checklists, Marketing Samples, Scripts, Forms, Paperwork, and detailed Training to conduct professionally.

26. Do *Deal Meeting*. Sign paperwork, **get Check!**

Steps 23, 24, 26 completed In-Person at Property when holding a "1-Hour Open House" *(see our detailed System)*

27. Schedule **Closing** with Buyer and your Attorney. Attorney gets Option Deposit, handles details.

28. If goal is to get cashed out soon, have Tenant Buyer **complete Applications** with Credit Repair Service and your Mortgage Broker. Review reports to estimate time for qualification.

29. Remove **Staging Kit** *(pics, plants, etc.)* from house.

30. Get non-owner occupied ("Landlord") Insurance.

31. Get **utilities**, electric/gas/water, set up with Buyer.

32. After Buyer moves in, deliver **gift basket** and ask for **Referrals** (offer Referral Gift/Bonus).

33. Maintain accounting spreadsheet for total business and individual properties.

34. Handle **Business Accounts**. Send and receive all Monthly Payments, maintain spreadsheet.

35. Provide ongoing **customer service** to Sellers and Lease Purchase Tenant Buyers. *(should be minimal)!*

*Now that we've gone through how **you'll** get started, we thought you might be curious how **we** got started in all this. We knew we had to include this fun and fascinating chapter in our lives when we got Ron to "volunteer" to tell HIS side of the story while we had a recorder rolling! Success Leaves Clues, so take note of smart Action Steps!*

Chapter 2
"How It All Began"

by Ron LeGrand

I remember it was a rainy day in Atlanta for my first ever "Millionaire Maker Boot Camp". I had recently parted ways with another company, and that whole mess had kept me off the road for the longest stretch in over 30 years. So it was a fresh start on my own again, I was pretty excited. I was getting back to doing what I loved, teaching real estate.

I noticed them pretty early on. They were sitting smack dab in the front row, bright and shiny on the first morning, big smiles on their faces. I knew right away they were weird.

As the morning went on I was feeling good. I had been exiled, and now I was finally free to teach again. The new manual I wrote was working well, and the students really seemed to be focused. Every time I glanced over at that weird couple they'd be nodding and grinning.

We got through to lunch, and I was actually enjoying myself. For a first-time event everything was going pretty smoothly. Then it happened, I got to the Role-Play section of the boot camp.

A good part of our training involves what to say to sellers, so I always include live role-playing. We act out a scenario where I'm the investor out at the sellers' house. So the second I asked for volunteers to role-play the sellers, what do you think happened? Was it any surprise?

The weird couple leaps up out of their chairs like they've been waiting for this moment their entire lives. They're almost to the stage before I even pick them. What am I supposed to do at that point, turn them away? The whole audience is already laughing, I think partly from surprise and partly from my obvious surprise.

Can you blame me? I'd been teaching for decades, and I'd never seen any volunteers show that kind of enthusiasm to get up on stage with me. I felt like Bob Barker on "The Price is Right". Looking back, that should've tipped me off right there. But I didn't heed the warning bells (as it turns out, thank goodness for that).

So I started with my normal lines, "Can I just take a look around? No dogs or naked people?" Yes that's what I say, it breaks the ice. So that gets a chuckle like normal, and we proceed to sit down. That's the last time the word "normal" could be applied to this particular Role Play.

I was going over the agreement like I'd done thousands of times before, and that's when it started. Now usually I get a couple meek questions, and I'm left hoping for a little more challenge. Here, every question and objection any seller has ever dreamed up started coming at me! I like a challenge, but I mean, there's a limit. Still, even though I was a little out of practice, I'm firing back all my best lines.

We've actually got a pretty good rhythm going, no sooner would I answer one question when they were right there with the next one. I started wondering where they were coming up with this stuff. All that was missing was the bright light shining in my eyes.

Fortunately I've been around long enough to have all the answers, even for the tough questions. And then the guy (Brian) asked a question I actually like: "We're not ready to move out yet, can we stay in the house a while?" That's a fairly common request in the Pretty House business, so guess what -- I created an agreement for that! I reached over and grabbed the manual, I showed all the students where the agreement was, and I explained this was the exact time when you would use it.

I set the manual back down, and I turned back to this weird couple. I asked if finally they were ready to sign, or if they had any truly last questions. The guy looks me right in the eye and asks with a totally straight face, "So, Ron...do you always bring that training manual out to the customer's houses with you?"

And here everything had been running so smoothly. This huge laugh erupts from the audience. I admit, even I had a chuckle at that one.

Then I came right back with, "No, but there's always one smartass in every crowd." The laughs went on for a while, and I sat looking across at this weird couple. I had this thought, and it was a feeling too, that maybe this could be the start of something. I had no idea.

The weird couple, Brian and Lynette Wolff as I came to find out, signed up for our Masters Program. I saw them at several events over the next 9 months, and they always came prepared.

This was back in the days when, believe it or not, I used an overhead projector to teach. The Wolffs would actually bring in color transparencies showing their house deals, complete with pictures and all the numbers. Brian went over the strategy, the deal structuring, and really told the story. He'd take questions like a pro, even though he was still fairly new at this. It didn't take me long to see he had some brains, and he was also a natural born teacher. I found out later he'd graduated *Summa Cum Laude*, and when we roasted the Wolff Couple last year one of the big laugh-getting punch lines was *"You're soo smart!"*

At the events Lynette would always chime in with all that bubbly energy. The students started calling her the Energizer Bunny, and that ain't far off. You know that saying about enthusiasm being contagious? If that's true, Lynette is *gosh dang viral!*

Every time Lynette grabbed the microphone from Brian and started talking everyone would start smiling. She wasn't just some bouncy cheerleader though, this was a woman with real accomplishments. I found out she actually set a state record when she sold 41 new homes in 1 month! I always got a special kick out of hearing these wise insights in that squeaky voice. Over the last decade and a half you don't know how many time I've heard that voice I love and hate, "Rooooon!"

Both Wolffs actually had extensive backgrounds in real estate before they came onto "Planet Ron". Lynette had been a #1 Realtor, and Brian was manager of an Ameriquest Mortgage office in downtown Phoenix, among other things. It didn't take me long to realize that this was quite a team.

We get hundreds of student testimonial letters at the office here in Jacksonville. When I read the Wolffs' letter I immediately told my assistant Donna to frame it and hang it in the lobby. I knew the Wolffs were in the Phoenix area, and I decided to see for myself what they were doing.

Lynette picked me up at the airport, and we drove straight to their big office. They gave me the grand tour, introduced me around to their staff, and showed me their impressive organization and automation systems.

Then we got to their scripts, and here again they were clearly on a whole other level. I found out that Brian had actually written movie scripts in Hollywood for 7 years! We talked about them helping out my other students with some of their scripts, maybe incorporating some of mine.

I saw the Wolffs at several of our events over the next few months. They always impressed me with their on- stage reports about deals they'd closed, and their ideas on the joint script system we'd talked about.

Around Halloween I found myself on stage with renowned Information Marketer and author (as well as a close colleague), Dan Kennedy. We were speaking at our Information Marketing Boot Camp, where we used to do a "Shark Tank" stage show before the TV show Shark Tank ever even existed.

We had students come up on stage and pitch their business ideas or product ideas to us. We'd offer our feedback, and all night it had not been pretty, nor kind. Neither of us have ever been the type to mince words.

So we were at the end of a very long line of presenters, and talk about slim pickings. All those pitches, and there wasn't a single one we liked! At this point there was actually kind of a depressing gloom over the room. We had one last chance, one lone name left on the list. Don't tell me – it's the Wolffs.

Of course when I called their names they jumped up and ran for the stage. They were even carrying some mocked up Manuals and DVDs with their pictures on them. Nobody else had anything like that. Weird.

So they took the microphone, and started talking. And talking, and walking, and talking. I looked out at the audience. They were all surprisingly engaged, even intent. What was going on? They weren't like this when anybody else was up on stage. Weird.

It wasn't just the way the Wolffs talked, they were obviously prepared and very enthusiastic. It was also what they talked about, they were passionate about this real estate investing script system. It looked like so much more than what we'd talked about!

They had taken the original simple idea of a "Script Kit", and created an entire all-encompassing Script, DVD, and CD package called "The

What to Say & What to Do" System. They even had a Forms CD and 3 good bonuses.

The Wolffs wrapped up their pitch, it was all quiet for a second, and then the place erupted with this thunderous applause. It was like the home team had just won on a last-second Hail Mary pass. Considering everyone who had presented before, I think it was just so unexpected. I must've been a little surprised too, because when the applause died out I couldn't immediately think of anything to say.

That's when my good friend and long-time colleague, Dan Kennedy, turned to me and said one word – *"Winner"*. Now I've known Dan for decades, and he's been right and he's been wrong. This time he got it 100% right.

The feedback from the audience was pretty amazing. They were actually asking the Wolffs for their phone number so they could buy the new system as soon as it was available. Suddenly it was fun to go through the audience responses again. The whole time Kennedy just sat there smiling. Every couple minutes he'd say "Winner" again.

Kennedy eventually explained to everyone how script systems have historically performed very well in the marketplace. He added some more encouraging words, and then, what do you think was the last thing he said? "Winner winner winner", his exact words, I swear.

Then Dan follows that with (to rousing applause), "Let's get Mr. & Mrs. Enthusiasm back up here!" To this day students love to refer to the Wolff Couple by that nickname, most without even knowing they got dubbed that by Dan Kennedy! Weird.

So the Wolffs did mention including my scripts in their "What to Say" System. It turns out Brian has a big background in TV, and now they wanted to shoot videos of everything I've ever said to every kind of seller and buyer.

No backing out now, I remember thinking. After all, it might be fun. Two long days later, I would look back wistfully at the moment I was thinking those things…

The Wolffs showed up at my house at 6:00 am, carrying massive cameras, lights, plus wardrobe and make-up for <u>fifteen</u> different characters!

They moved around everything in my office, then everything in the dining room, then everything in the living room. When they turned on those bright movie lights I thought I'd either gone blind, or gone to heaven!

Then we started shooting the Closing Call Role Plays, and I realized right away Brian knew what he was doing in front of and behind the camera. Sometimes he was wearing a crazy wig or moustache, but he always knew what he wanted and how to get it as a Director.

I actually found myself calling him *"Mr. Director"*! As you may know about me, I don't listen to a lot of people, and I sure as heck don't let anyone boss me around and tell me what to do (especially not a man). Well, I guess there's a first time for everything.

It wasn't a mystery why I should go along with his direction, and even agree to do second or third takes. I could tell we were recording some truly ground-breaking, money-making training here. A thought even occurred to me, that what we were creating that day was historic.

Now, after generating millions in revenue and millions in students' profits, history has proven me right about the "What to Say" System. I could tell it would be like gold to the students…and of course it is, it contains plenty of 24-karat Ron!

For 2 whole days in a dozen different locations we Role-Played real estate investing scenarios, and filmed it all to play for thousands of knowledge-hungry investors.

It was just like when we'd Role-Played that first time on stage in Atlanta, only this time it was for the cameras, as well as for the generations of students to follow. And yes, they asked every question and objection just like they did before, only this time they got to write them down in advance.

Over those shooting days we essentially captured on video the real estate investing business. Me, Brian, Lynette, and a camera crew… longest 2 days of my life.

The system we ended up creating together actually exceeded everyone's expectations, even mine. The very first time the Wolffs offered the "What to Say & What to Do" System from stage in San Diego, they broke every record by selling 35 systems!

They continue to stay on the cutting edge with the smartest training out there. There's nobody better to teach you key areas like what to say, marketing, selling houses fast, and getting an Acquisitionist. They touch on all those areas in this book as well. Now they've gone on to teach alongside me all across America for over 15 years.

Over those years I've watched the Wolffs close countless deals for our students, from leads the students brought to the live events themselves. If I had one great seller lead and I wanted the best chance to turn it into a deal, I'd hand it over to the Wolffs. I don't know what could be a better testament to their skill than that (of course they learned it from me).

Now after all these years, I finally got the Wolffs to write a book. It's just like all their systems, it far exceeds expectations!

This book is like a whole real estate training course right in your hands. I was so impressed with the amount of detail here, especially the checklists, forms, and money-making scripts.

Even if you have no experience, even if you have no cash and no credit, this book gives you a real chance to close a Creative Financing Deal. Buying this book may be the least expensive, most important thing you ever do!

I have great respect for the Wolffs professionally, and personally we've grown to be truly close friends. For over 15 years now we've worked side-by-side on stages in major cities all across America, teaching our students how to make real money in real estate investing.

For almost that long we've gallivanted together all around the globe, living life to the fullest. I count myself lucky to have had these folks beside me on stage and in life for all these years.

If you want my best advice, get them on your side too. You won't find any better teachers of real estate investing, or anybody who cares more about your personal success.

You know...maybe it's not such a bad thing to be a little weird after all.

Good Luck, & Good Investing!
-Ron LeGrand

Mike Maddox - *Covington, LA*

This is me holding a check for **$16,660.25**. I nailed this deal down while I was in the field, sleeping on a cot, with caveman internet and almost zero cell coverage. If that ain't determination, I don't know what is!

More good news: I've got another closing next week that should net about $6500 and **3 more deals** on the way this month. I am really on a roll now and it feels incredible!! My wife has really been supportive as well. So much so, she was behind me 100% when I decided to QUIT MY JOB and do this full time. She has jumped on this success train with me and not looked back.

Next stop... Financial Freedom. We make a great team, she helps keep us organized and focused. Thanks for sticking with me while I was away for weeks and months at a time on duty. I knew once things slowed down I was going to become an overnight real estate NINJA. Just kidding, lol. I have much to learn. So I'll just continue to work extra hard and sponge up all of the wonderful knowledge and wisdom you guys are kind enough to bestow on this humble entrepreneur.

By the way; the mental shift that happens when you get your first big check is something that cannot be truly understood until it happens to you. It unlocks your potential and paves the way for future successes. The Law of Attraction is strong at work in my life, and **all the glory for my achievements go to God**. He has guided my hand, given me wisdom, kept my heart in the right place, and allowed me to cross paths with you. **I am forever grateful.**

Kent Palmer - Janesville, WI

I have chills running down my spine as I am typing this to you guys because I am so excited. As a result of your direction and encouragement to take action, I had a **$37,000.00 payday today**!!! I placed a Pretty House under a Sandwich Lease Option Purchase Contract and found a happy tenant buyer who gave me a non-refundable option deposit of $37,000.00!!!!!!!! I had a total of approximately **two hours involved** in this deal to make that kind of money; **I am hooked for life**, you're going to see a lot more of me around. I was thinking, I use to work for 16 years as a Juvenile Detention Officer with a college degree and made around $39,000 per year, and that's before taxes. I **netted more in one day than I made in 1 year** at my past occupation; isn't that crazy?! This couldn't have came at a better time, with the loss of my girlfriend's sister and taking in her daughter, I am able to pay off all the funeral expenses and other unexpected costs due to her passing. **I will never forget the first day I met you guys** at the Boot Camp in California and Brian encouraging me to sign up with your Mentoring Program; the best thing I ever did! Oh, I did not have the money by the way! When I got back home, I borrowed it from my Dad and guess what, yup, he is paid off now!!!

Chapter 3
Getting Started On the Fast Track

Read the following, aloud if possible:
I Desire Real Estate Riches.
I want the Freedom that Wealth will bring.
I've made up my mind to do this.
I Expect Success.
I am Committed to Success.
My Mind tells me, "I can do this!"
Now here's where I learn **how to get started!**

You want to **change your life** through Real Estate Investing. To understand where to start, you must **understand your Goals**. Approach investing intelligently, with a real **Business Plan**, and it will reward you like very few businesses can. A crucial part of your Business Plan are your Goals. I love the word "**Ac<u>cou</u>ntable**". You want **numerical targets** so you can "count" your progress, and **track your results**.

REALISTIC GOALS FOR A NEW INVESTOR

When setting your initial Goals many factors come into play.

First off, are you starting part time, or full time? _____ Most of our students get going while they're still working another job. That must work if Real Estate Investing is going to serve as an **Exit Strategy from the rat race**. You can't (and shouldn't) quit your current income source until you can **replace it** with another. That new income source must also be *dependable*. So where should you set your Goals as you establish your new profitable enterprise?

Remember in our personal case (and maybe in yours) there were two considerable incomes to replace. We were looking for something big. As we came to discover, the world of **Creative Financing is BIG**. When properly systemized, the income potential can **exceed your wildest dreams**, not to mention your **actual numerical targets**.

Your Goals are most effective when they're **written or typed**, and **posted** in a conspicuous spot.

It's also important to have **Deadlines**. Goals without Plans and Deadlines are just wishes. Set numerical targets. We like to actually set Goals with a Minimum and Optimum, as you can see in this chart. These numbers are excellent guidelines for you, and even the minimum goal would make you **pretty rich** pretty quickly. **Commit to hitting at least the minimums,** and if you find a rewarding Marketing Method you might just surprise yourself with your results.

Creative Financing Action Step	# of Units Minimum Monthly Goal	# of Units Optimum Monthly Goal
Market for **Leads**	25	60
Closing Calls	20	50
Deal Meetings	4	8
Signed Deals	1	4
Open Houses	1	2
Open House Tenant Buyer Leads	10	80
Tenant Buyers Installed	1	4
TOTAL Deals	1	4

What It Takes to Succeed

We love lists, even very short ones, so here we have 4 for you as short as could be (and still qualify as "lists"). These are deceptively vital **Keys to Success,** so they are important to be aware of when you are starting out. Please look them over, think them over, and take them to heart. You will thank us.

2 Keys to Success in Real Estate Investing
1. **Commitment** - measured in minutes/dollars
2. **Training** - find and work with the best

2 More Keys to Success in Real Estate Investing
1. **Make a Schedule** - 7-10 hrs/week
2. **Stick to the Schedule** - print & post

2 *More* Keys to Success in Real Estate Investing
1. **Systems** - Follow Detailed Plans & Checklists
2. **Scripts** - Find Proven Versions, Stick to them!

2 *More* Keys to Success in Real Estate Investing
1. **Consistent Lead Flow** -- Marketing!
2. **Timely Closing Calls** -- Get on Phone!

The next pages feature your **"Fast Start Checklist"**, this is vital to follow closely as you're getting going.

Fast Start Checklist

1. Get Trained – *find someone good, or go to **the best***
2. Decide on your Business Name – *professional, credible*
3. Research and Reserve your Business Name at your State's Corporate Commission website or location
4. Form Business Entity (LLC best in most states) through State Corporate Commission website or location
5. Buy *YourBusinessName*.com, or buy good Marketing URL for your website address – *.com, catchy, short, easy to spell*
6. Get Business Phone – *add phone to existing plan*
7. Order Business Cards featuring phone number & website
8. Post Website – *same information as on Business Cards*
9. Set Up Office – *laptop, printer, 3 file racks, file box/drawer, manila folders, legal & letter sized paper, legal-size portfolio*
10. Create and Post Schedule – 7-10 hours/week, *or more*
11. Print Documents to Prepare **5** Buying Packets – *insert into manila folders*
12. Print Documents to Prepare **5** Selling Packets – *insert into manila folders*
13. Put 2 Buying & 2 Selling Packets in Legal-Size Portfolio *be ready professionally & mentally for Deal Meetings*
14. Review and print important Forms – *FSBO Call Script, Closing Call Prep Sheet, 50 Closing Calls Checklist, etc.*
15. Write Real Estate Investor Bio – *2-3 lines, 10-30 seconds*
16. Choose "Farm Area" – *buyers like area, but not too hot*
17. Make Marketing Plan – *use Marketing Tracking Chart*
18. Implement Marketing Plan – *takes a little focus & money* FSBO Caller, internet marketing, business cards, etc.
19. Practice reading all Scripts aloud – *even better, Role Play*
20. Start making Closing Calls, set Appointments
21. Go out to Sellers' houses for Deal Meetings
22. Maintain Focus on your Goals, Track your Progress.

CONTINUING ACTION STEP AREAS

At the start the 2 things your investing business must build to be successful are <u>Foundation</u> and <u>Momentum</u>.

This book is the perfect guide to help you set up your Foundation. Follow all the Action Steps on the previous page and you'll soon build momentum. As you progress you'll get more and more comfortable every day in your role of successful Real Estate Investor.

Now the **key is consistency**. You need to stick to the Schedule that you committed to, at least **7-10 hours** per week. You'll make constant adjustments to your schedule, but always remember that your **schedule is the lifeline of your business**. If you're not there moving your business forward, it's not moving forward (until you hire your first assistant, which makes a lot of financial and common sense ASAP—refer to our "Acquisitionist System").

Once you have your Foundation and Momentum, your activities will break down into the following 4 areas. Don't neglect any of them, or your Momentum will be adversely affected. These activities will grow your successful real estate investing business. You now have the power to make good decisions about what needs to be focused on and when.

1. Ongoing Training

- **Keep reading this book,** there is so much depth here.
- Contact our office to set a time for a **Goal-Planning Session with the Wolff Couple!** This is a very special offer for book-owners only. You can come to us in Arizona, or we can do your Goals and Planning on the phone via Skype or Facetime. Call to get going on that, very important, at **888-Rich-Now!**
- **CALL IN on our "Teaching Tuesdays" Conference Call** at 7 pm ET/4pm PT! We cover a new and exciting topic every

week, all designed to **make you smarter** and **make you money!** Many of our students say this is the **most important hour** of their entire week!

- **Watch** our awesome, **professional videos** at **YouTube.com/WolffCouple**, and **subscribe** to be notified of new posts . You can even catch up on prior seasons of our amazing video clip series, **"Wolff Bite" Wednesdays!** Don't miss our new posting each week!

- Catch us on our weekly **"Facebook LIVE Thursdays"** at 7 pm ET/4 pm PT! That's an easy and terrific way to **stay connected** with us, and continually get the most cutting edge training (and fun stuff too) for FREE!

2. Marketing

- **Don't ever stop** marketing, for both sellers and buyers!
- **Keep Track** of your marketing efforts and what is working best for you on the "Marketing Tracking Chart".
- Continue to use the **"FSBO Call Script"** and the **"Landlord Script"** to call on ads and any signs you see.
- We've given you Marketing information here, yet you should consider getting a more complete system, such as our **Wolff-LeGrand "Masterful Marketing" System"**. It contains not only all of **Ron's marketing wisdom**, gained over his decades of experience in this business, but a ton more **Training from us**, and also additional **proven Marketing Samples in digital form.**

3. Doing Deals

- Market enough to get **25-60 Leads** per month.
- Keep having FSBO Caller or You do **Opening Calls**
- Keep making **20-50 Closing Calls** per month

- Do **4-8 Deal Meetings**, and get **Signed Agreements!**
- Just follow all the **powerful scripts** in our systems and this book. When you find a motivated seller or a qualified buyer make the appointment, and try to **close the deal ASAP**. Time is always of the essence.

4. Taking Care of Business

- To keep your office & business in good working order, follow the form "Steps of Deal Organization". Keep track of your deals in progress on your computer with the "Deal Organization Chart" and on paper with our "D.U.F.U.S." Lead Organization System. If you have not yet received these from us, just email us at WolffCouple@gmail.com
- Keep the right Step-by-Step Checklist and a Comment Log in each file, and whenever you do anything on the file make sure to **update them** by writing in the date that the step was completed.
- Follow the **Step by Step Checklists** to make sure you always know <u>What to Do</u>!

IN EARLIER **STEP BY STEP CHECKLISTS** REMEMBER SOMEONE NEEDS TO DO ALL STEPS, BUT IT DOESN'T HAVE TO BE YOU! USE AN ACQUISITIONIST AS MUCH AS YOU CAN (SEE OUR **"ACQUISITIONIST" SYSTEM)**.

Chapter 4
Masterful Marketing
Finds Motivated Sellers!

The **Success or Failure of your Marketing Plan**
will mean the **Life or Death** of your new business.

That's a **strong statement**, isn't it? It's also a pretty cold observation. Almost kind of scary. That would imply that **this should be the most important** section of the book. Here's what a truly masterful Marketer, **Ron LeGrand**, has to say about it:

"Marketing is the **#1 Step**. We have to find people with a house for sale and **get them to call us**. If we miss that step, **the rest is irrelevant**. If you don't find people who want to do business with you, pretty soon you won't be in business.

Spend more time on Marketing, and you'll find the rest of the business **becomes a lot easier**. Obviously Marketing is the **first thing** you need to do, but really it's **the most important thing**.

Because without it, there's nothing else to do.

So spend some time and a little bit of money and effort locating prospects. Get the phone flooding with calls, and focus on the few that want to do business with you. That's how you start to **make millions on Creative Financing Deals**. Just do what the Wolffs teach you to do, and you'll be fine."

- Ron LeGrand

The real **bottom line of Marketing** is, *are you fin ding enough flexible sellers?* You don't need many.

Put out enough Marketing to attract **1** flexible seller per month. Talk to them on the phone to work out a good Purchase Price, Monthly Payment, Term, and Down Payment *(none)*. These are the 4 Pretty House Deal Points.

Go see the house and get the paperwork signed. It's that simple. So often we are bound and determined to overcomplicate things, especially you "Thinker Brains" (don't be offended, I'm one of the tribe)!

You'll realize how simple it is the first time you do it yourself. Any imagined fears you're harboring will fade quickly as the deal comes together and your tenant buyer hands you a big check. Just do that once a month, and you will get rich.

It's That Simple!

So simple, yet absolutely vital. That's why we are devoting such a large section to Marketing!

So what are the best ways to attract sellers? Marketing for Real Estate Investing includes ***14 Main Marketing Methods***. These include everything from Business Cards to Internet Ads, from Roadside Signs to Letters, and everything in between. We'll get into those Methods in detail, but let's start with the big picture.

THE
4 GREAT
PRINCIPLES
OF MARKETING!

Marketing Principle #1
Marketing is First and Foremost!

Your Marketing Plan and Methods should always be the primary consideration of your business.

To be successful a business needs revenue, and you won't make a dollar in any business until you find customers who want your product or service. That is the task of your Marketing, to find enough "Suspects" to uncover the few "Prospects" you need each month.

Marketing brings these customers, and customers are the lifeblood of any business. Without customers who want what you're offering, you have no business! That's why *Marketing is First and Foremost!*

Your goal is to talk with at least 20 people (and hopefully as many as 50 or more) with a house for sale each month. You'll also need to talk to that many Buyers, or possibly many more. The key with Buyers is how fast and automated the house-selling process is with our "1-Hour Sale" System.

One key aspect of Real Estate Investing is that, unlike most businesses, you only need to find 1-3 Sellers and 1-3 Buyers per month to become very wealthy.

Marketing Principle #2
Trial & Error Is Vital.

To generate reliable revenue each month you need to find 20-50 potential Sellers, and probably 20-80+ potential Buyers. Some combination of the _14 Main Marketing Methods_ will consistently provide these Prospects. You just need to figure out exactly what will be your winning combination! You need to "crack that code", and through what process? Through _Trial & Error_, of course!

We'll be showing you in great detail in our Step- by-Step sections how to implement some of the _Main Marketing Methods_. As you _take action_ you will get specific results. A certain number of Sellers and Buyers will respond to your Marketing Messages.

If you've never marketed for Home Sellers and Buyers before then obviously there will be a "Learning Curve". By tracking your results carefully you can really accelerate that learning curve. You can quickly figure out which Methods are getting you the best response, and finding you the qualified Prospects that you need to succeed.

3 Steps to Trial & Error Success

1. **Implement 3-4 Marketing Methods** with histories of Success -- _Follow our Directions carefully_

2. **Track Your Results** – _Use Marketing Tracking Chart_

3. **Make Smart Adjustments** – _Stop doing_ what doesn't get results, and _do more of_ what **does** get results.

We teach all about **Making Smart Adjustments** in your business AND your life at our amazing…

When it's your business and your Marketing money on the line, you need to **know your results** so you can make those **game-changing smart adjustments**. That's the only way you can take advantage of the Principle of *Trial & Error*. A great way to track your results is to use the *Marketing Tracking Form* included in this book.

Marketing Principle #3
It's a Numbers Game.

For every Marketing Method you try, you will get a certain response. Through *Trial & Error* you'll figure out where the most and the best leads are coming from. Then it's just a matter of scale, of increasing or decreasing the amount of Messages you are getting out into the Marketplace. The more Messages, the more Marketing Pieces, the higher response.

It's a Numbers Game!

If you send out 500 letters to a list, you will get a certain response. If you send 1000 letters to the same list, you will most likely get double the response. So it's simple, if you're not getting enough leads you need to distribute a higher number of Marketing pieces.

You need to get out more signs or letters or flyers, or whatever other Marketing Methods you choose. No matter what, **you need to commit** to doing whatever it takes to get the number of Prospects you need to succeed.

That being said, you want to (and maybe *need* to) be careful with your Marketing Budget. You may want to get our system, "Target Marketing on Any Budget". It actually provides you with over a dozen pre-structured Marketing Plans, with budgets on each of them from $100 - $1000 per month. This is extremely helpful when deciding on your own monthly Marketing Plan.

You don't need to spend a lot of money on Marketing, though we have students who regularly spend many thousands per month. Our students who own Homevestor franchises can spend $10K/month or more. Then we have some students who spend less than $100. It's unusual to spend more than $1000 per month, unless you are doing tons of letters, radio, TV, or Internet (Facebook) Ads. Just remember that when you double the amount of Messages, you double the cost <u>and</u> you also double the return!

So when you find a Marketing Method that produces, you can just turn the leads on and off like a faucet with your Marketing dollars.

<u>Marketing Principle #4</u>
Consistency is Crucial.

You need to maintain focus on your Real Estate Marketing and really **stay consistent!** You can't dally around with a little here and a little there, and just hope that deals will drop into your lap.

Each month you need to decide on your Marketing Plan (sample Plans are in your "Target Marketing" System), and then apply it consistently. f you want consistent results, it's simple, you must keep Marketing consistently.

Many of the responses to your Marketing will NOT be from the Prospect's first exposure to your Message. Depending on the Marketing Method, it may be the 2nd or 5th or even 10th time they've seen it before they are finally compelled to contact you.

This is true for many Methods such as Business Cards, and it's especially true for Roadside Signs. Signs always work for Buyers, but the first couple times you put out Seller signs it might seem like they don't quite register with the public. Then after your signs have been out there for 1 or 2 months (or 6 or 12), the quality calls really start coming in.

It's highly unlikely you'll ever get 50 Seller Incoming Calls per month just off Roadside Signs. If you can get 10-20 that would be awesome! These are usually high quality leads that pay off with a high Conversion Ratio.

In fact, 6 out of our first 10 deals came from Roadside Signs. That's all **because of Lynette!** In the beginning she always made sure to set her alarm for 5:30 am every Saturday, so she could make sure to roll over and kick me out of bed to go put out 50 signs! *Lynette did her part!*

I was very focused at the start, and I personally put out about 200 signs every month. Of course I was carefully monitoring all our results for *Trial & Error* purposes. It struck me how it took a while for the phone to start ringing, but pretty soon Roadside Signs turned into one of our most reliably producing Marketing Methods.

So even if the response starts a little slow on some Methods, give them a chance. Keep getting the right Marketing Messages through the right Media in the right amount to the right people, and *the response will come!*

There you have it, you'll profit more by remembering…

THE
4 GREAT
PRINCIPLES
OF MARKETING!

Now we're going to be honored by the wise words of a true **Guru of Real Estate Investing, Ron LeGrand.** We met Ron over 15 years ago, and he proceeded to absolutely and irrevocably **change our lives** for the better.

Ron's bought **over 3000 homes**, and he's still investing today. More than **half a million people** have attended his trainings, and he's the **nation's leading authority** on Creative Financing/Pretty House Deals.

Folks love Ron for his "straight-talking" Southern style, and admire him for his expertise on all matters Real Estate. He's the man who first showed us **the path to our success** in Creative Financing Deals!

Since then we've grown to be great friends, we teach on-stage together at a couple dozen events every year, and we even go on vacation together. Last year we took one cruise to Cuba, and another to Australia, Tasmania, and New Zealand. Soon we'll be in Europe together on a Rhine River Cruise!

Ever since we met Ron our Real Estate Investing Business has exploded, and we've branched off in so many directions, including writing this book. We've become millionaires, we've done over 700 house deals, and the snowball really got rolling with...**Marketing!**

That's how we found our first Seller, and our first Buyer. That's how we made our first Non-Refundable Option Deposit for a whopping $9000!

I'll tell you, it doesn't seem like so much now, but that $9000 was the **biggest and sweetest paycheck** I had ever seen in my life. It wasn't even the cash so much, it was what it symbolized too me.

It meant that **a new life** was opening up to me, Lynette, and our family. Where there had been gloom, the horizon ahead suddenly looked so bright. I truly believed it then, and it has come to pass since. We really **got our life back!**

What is at the very foundation of our success, and has sustained our life-changing Real Estate Investing Business all the way to today, is **Marketing!**

Now we work with our family and "Acquisitionists" to make big money on Autopilot, and really live our dreams!

All Thanks to Marketing!

So let's hear from our great Mentor and close friend, Ron LeGrand. Get ready for Ron's **business acumen, practical advice**, and **homespun wisdom** on the timeless subject of Marketing -- specifically **Marketing to find Creative Financing Deals!**

KEY POINTS OF MARKETING

by Ron LeGrand

The **1st Step** to being a successful real estate entrepreneur is to **Locate Prospects**, and that means **Marketing**. If you don't find people who want to do business with you, pretty soon you won't be in business. I've been in business for over 50 years now, over 30 of it in real estate and the rest in other businesses. I learned a long time ago that the 1st Step is finding someone who wants your product or service.

Marketing is the **#1 Step**. In real estate, <u>we have to find people who have a house for sale</u> and get them to call us. If we miss that step, the rest is irrelevant.

Spend more time on Marketing, and you'll find the rest of the business becomes **a lot easier**. Obviously it's the first thing you need to do, but really it's **the most important thing**. *Because without it, there's nothing else to do.*

In any business if you get people coming in exchanging their money for your product or service, that's always exciting. When you can do it better than most anybody else who you're competing with, that's also exciting. Because with all this powerful Marketing Training right here, you have the knowledge to get people to respond to your message. You really don't have any competition, because they're just totally ignorant about marketing for the most part.

In our world of real estate, gosh, we can only handle one or two houses a month anyway. We only need one buyer per house, so it's not like we have to drive in thunderous herds. It's really simply a funnel. Bring in the suspects in the top, prescreen them quickly down to the prospects, and take those out of that little pile at the bottom that are now going to do business with you.

Pick the low-hanging fruit! And that, what I just described, is **the way all businesses work.**

I've talked to so many students over the years, and I find that when they're having a problem within their business, it's usually that they **didn't locate enough prospects.** In other words, they didn't crank up the buying machine and get people with a house for sale to call them. They're trying to do business with 1 or 2 or 3 prospects they got this month, and that's just not going to cut it.

The majority of the people who call will be suspects. <u>The minority are going to be prospects</u>. Spend some time and a little bit of money and effort locating prospects. <u>Get the phone flooding with calls</u>, then you'll find the rest of the business becomes very easy.

I want your readers to be getting at least 10, 15, 20 calls per month from sellers. Frankly, <u>if you're not getting at least 15 - 20 calls a month</u> from sellers, <u>your buying mac hine is broke</u>. You need to fix it.

There's 3 very important things in Marketing; Message, Market, & Media. Our message is simple: We Buy Houses! We can buy them quick. We can do it painlessly. We can get you out and you can walk away today.

Our market is obviously people who have a house for sale. And then our media is the 14 Marketing Methods. <u>The key is getting the right message to the right market</u>. If we are successful in doing that, we can get a lot less calls and make a lot more money out of each one.

I don't think you need to spend more than $1,000 per month on Marketing. I have students making over a million dollars a year that don't spend more than $1,000 per month driving sellers to them.

Pick 3 or 4 of the things that you want to use. <u>You need 3 or 4 things</u> <u>working</u>. The key is <u>you've got to get stuff out there c ontinually</u> <u>working</u>. You can't just stick your toe in the water and learn how to swim.

Sometimes you're going to have to change the things you do. Sometimes it's not right. Sometimes you make a mess out of it, because you didn't get the right message at the right time.

You just hang in there and keep the messages that are working working, and change the stuff that's not working. Keep an eye on what you're spending where, and it won't take you long to **figure out what works best** for you where you live. And I'll be the first to admit that some things work better in other areas than they do in your area.

That's called **Trial and Error**. Well, actually I've never made any mistakes in my marketing whatsoever. At least, not so far today that I can recall.

You Wolffs have a great **Marketing Tracking Chart** right here in this book. You give your readers the ability to keep track of what they're spending on what media, and measure the results so they can quickly determine what works and what doesn't. Pretty soon we'll arrive at the 2 or 3 or 4 things that we want to use that make the most sense -- <u>the biggest bang for the buck</u>. It's our responsibility as entrepreneurs to get the biggest bang for our marketing buck that we can get.

When it all comes down to it, <u>it's a very simple</u> <u>process</u>. Find out what people want. Find a way to get the message to them, and give them the choice of whether they want to respond or not. The exact same thing holds true with people who have houses for sale.

Let's look at the basics of Marketing: #1, all your marketing messages must have what's in it for me within the message. People could care less about you. They care about them. So all your marketing messages should clearly state why I should do business or **why I should call you**.

That's another very important point. The purpose of a business card is not to sell anything. The purpose of a sign, a flyer, an ad is not to sell anything. It's strictly to get a customer to call you. What happens when they call you is what makes the sale happen.

What has to be in your Marketing Method is a **triggering mechanism** to get the customer to respond. That's called a Unique Selling Proposition. A **"U.S.P."**

Make sure that you accomplish **W.I.I.F.M.**, **W**hat's In It **F**or **M**e. Just remember that radio station, WIIFM. Unique Selling Propositions like "We Buy Houses", "Sell Your House Today", "Sell Fast for Top Price", or whatever. All Marketing Media must have an Attention Grabbing Mechanism in order to get the customer's attention.

What I love about Marketing is that if you do it correctly it **generates a lot of revenue**. If you got to spend a few dollars on your Marketing Budget, it's totally irrelevant to the amount of revenue that you can get back on the other end, which is unlike most businesses.

I have restaurants, we have to spend money to get money and we don't get any $20,000 paychecks! None. So it's totally different world. If I got to spend a few dollars to mail letters or pay a FSBO Caller or whatever, it's totally irrelevant to the amount of profit that I can get back on the other end, which is unlike most businesses.

So this thing called Creative Financing is not like most businesses. We put almost no money out and we get back big, big chunks with no risk. No risk. It's a beautiful thing.

Just get your Marketing out there. Do what the Wolffs and I have taught you to do right here, and before you know it the **prospects and the cash will be pouring in!**

Good Luck & Good Investing!
- Ron LeGrand

THE 14 MARKETING METHODS

1. Business Cards – Professional and Marketing Cards
2. Internet Marketing – Zillo, Facebook, Craigslist, +
3. Website – must drive traffic to it for good results
4. Roadside Signs – Bit of a Pain, Reliably Productive
5. Outbound Calls – Mandatory Method for Beginners, Call Zillow, Craigslist, other FSBO Leads
6. Vehicle Signs – Full Wraps to removable Door Magnets
7. Classified Ads – On-line & Newspaper/Magazine
8. Postcards – less expensive Direct Mail
9. Letters Target Lists:
   Pre-Foreclosure – best sent in a series
   Out-of-State Owners – often productive mailing list
   Expired Listings Letters – get listings from
   Realtor 90 Day + Listings Letters – very targeted
10. Flyers/Door Hangers – a favorite method
11. Customer Referrals – warm leads = high conversion
12. Ant Farm – get others driving for dollars for YOU
13. Realtors – know about deals, not paid unless YOU paid
14. Advanced Methods – TV, Radio, Billboards, etc.

Over the next pages we'll expand on the **TOP 5 Marketing Methods** to start out with. We'll have the experts – Ron LeGrand, Lynette Wolff, and Brian Wolff – giving their individual Key Points on each one!

QUICK START MARKETING PLAN

With the proven samples in this book you can really get your marketing and your business going. Please be aware that we have an entire home Action Step System on Marketing for sellers, complete with digital versions of all the marketing samples here, and lots more great training from us and Ron.

**If you'd like more information on our
"Masterful Marketing with Ron LeGrand"
System please contact our office at 888-Rich-Now.**

Always track your marketing efforts and results on the Marketing Tracking Chart. This will help you to create and implement the most effective marketing campaigns possible.

Review the 14 Marketing Methods, choose 3-5 to start with, and write them down here. Soon you'll learn through Trial and Error which work the best for you.

You should definitely be passing out 3 business cards (mentioning a $350 referral fee) to everyone you see during the day, so we've filled that one in for you already. It's also easy and free to put ads on CraigsList and other Internet sites, so everyone should be consistently running ads there (remember you need to refresh them often to stay near the top). Sample cards can be found in a few pages.

Marketing Method #1 - Business Cards

_____

_____

Marketing Method #2 - Outbound Calls to FSBOs

_____

_____

Marketing Method #3 - Internet Ads / CraigsList

_____

_____

Marketing Method #4

_____

_____

Marketing Method #5

_____

_____

Marketing Method #6

_____

_____

1. Business Cards – Professional and Marketing Cards

RON'S KEY POINTS

Business Cards are a Method you add to your marketing toolbox, and you <u>hand them out everywhere you go</u>. The purpose of a business card is not to sell anything. The purpose of a sign, a flyer, an ad is not to sell anything. It's <u>strictly to get a customer to call you</u>. What has to be in that business card is a triggering mechanism to get the customer to respond. That's called a <u>Unique Selling Proposition</u>. A "U.S.P."

In fact, I would suggest that all of our listeners go to the system and pick out a card they like and adapt it to their needs. <u>Don' t try to reinvent the marketing wheel</u> that we already know is successful.

The more you can telegraph of what's in it for me onto this card, the better chance that customer's got of calling you. So, you <u>never waste the bac k</u> . For a few pennies more, you can use the back and the front.

The front is simply to drive them to the back. So I want a good, strong message on it, and I want a card that is easily recognizable and grabs attention.

Never use all caps. All caps are hard to read. Now, there's a couple words like cash and free that work with all caps, but for the most part, no matter what kind of advertising you do, signs, posters, flyers, cards, whatever, never use all caps. It'd just be hard to read. It should be big, bold, black, easy-to-read words. Don't get creative here.

We're going to get some bright cards. If we're going to go to bright colors, let's make them bright colors, not boring colors. Now a lot of people will settle for these, because their printers don't have the kind of paper in stock when they walk in the door. Any printer can order fluorescent c olored paper . It costs a little bit more, but it's worth it.

And, that's another thing. Forget about what these c ards cost. It's what they're costing you if they don't get done and they don't get out that's important.

What do you do with these cards? Here' s the key— distribute them. It's a secret. Get them out of the box and get them out. **Everywhere you go,** the cards must be left. Restaurants, give them to waiters. Put them on top of their urinals so the guys can grab them when they go. Pin them up the bulletin boards. Send them in your bills when you mail out your bills to local people.

Hand them out. Get them out everywhere. Make it a habit to get out at least 10 business cards a day. I promise you if you do that, you will buy at least 5 or 6 houses a year from these little old cheap business cards.

LYNETTE'S KEY POINTS
Face-to-face contact in Marketing is awesome. That's what makes business cards so special. Plus you can give them out anywhere, any-

time, to anybody! The response can be enthusiastic and immediate! That person or someone they know may have a house for sale. And if they don't, you mention your juicy finder's fee for the future.

Business cards can be FUN! You get to talk to people about what you're doing, and let your enthusiasm and excitement shine through. You are out there offering people a great solution, and they'll thank you for it!

BRIAN'S KEY POINTS

This is one of the least expensive and yet most under-used **Marketing Methods** of all. You just choose the text for your card from the samples provided, order them from the printer, and soon they are in your possession.

As Ron says, the cards don't do anyone any service in the box. You need to distribute a high number of these inexpensive Marketing pieces. Whether you bump into someone you know, or you meet someone new, or you interface with anyone throughout your day. This can include your dry-cleaner, any server at a restaurant, anybody and everybody!

We have detailed techniques for dispersal, so you can process large volumes of cards. You can talk to store managers in your Farm Area, and acquire permission to leave 20-30 cards in a holder on the counter. Then go back in to check on them, and remind the manager of your referral fee. With that approach you can disseminate 200-300 messages into the field every month if not more.

We Buy & Sell Houses

Your Company Name

Your Name(s)

Owner/Managers

Pretty or Ugly, Any Area! Buyers--Bad Credit OK
No Commissions, No Closing Costs, No Hassles!
<u>Sell Now</u> — Call 555-555-5555
<u>Buy Now</u> — Call 555-555-5555

<u>BACK</u>

When you need to <u>Sell</u> or <u>Buy</u>, we are the <u>EZ</u> Answer!
NO Commissions, NO Closing Costs, NO Hassles!
We buy houses in ANY area & ANY condition, but you don't
have to be a "distressed" Seller — We often pay FULL price!
We can even buy your house if you owe <u>more</u> than it's worth.
You may be late on payments, the house may need repairs,
we take care of everything to make it fast and easy!
We have <u>Great Rent-to-Own Homes</u> too — Bad Credit OKAY!
Get a nice home now, or get a deal on a Sweat Equity home!

Call us at 000-000-0000

YourWebsite.com

(Pass this card to someone we help, and we pay you $350!)

The Business Card here is first to pass out to any personal or professional contacts you have, making sure folks in your social circles know you are looking to buy and sell houses. Many of our students' first deals came from people that they knew, or who knew someone trying to sell. With these "warm" referrals you've already overcome the "Can I trust you?" objection. If the numbers work, many times someone you know can quickly lead to your first deal!

You'll also use this Professional card, which is similar to an attractive Realtor's card, with your sellers and buyers. You'll use the next "Marketing" Card, with a fluorescent front and black and white back, to distribute around your Farm Area -- leave on counters, post on bulletin boards, etc...

2. Internet Marketing – Zillow, Facebook, Craigslist, etc.

BRIAN

The Internet as a Marketing Medium has truly taken off in the last 10 years. At minimum you should currently be using **Zillow, Craigslist,**

and Facebook. Beyond that you could be using other "For Sale By Owner" websites, Real Estate websites, even eBay.

A huge amount of this Marketing is FREE. You may also want to post **Facebook Ads**, with which you can specifically target geographic and demographic groups (such as "likely to move"), but that does cost some money.

A worthwhile Facebook Ad Posting will probably cost you anywhere from a hundred up to maybe a thousand dollars. Of course you can spend a lot more than that, but make sure you are getting results before the costs get too high. You can also get involved and post your Messages in Facebook Groups, which is free but you need to exercise a little caution with that.

To get a lot more crucial information and all the detailed steps you need for this entire Marketing Method, just refer to our **"Internet Marketing" System with Cale Wolff.** Cale is our son, of course, and a total computer whiz! He got a full scholarship to the ASU Honors College for Computer Science. Just **call our office at 888-Rich-Now!**

3. Website – must drive traffic to it for good results

RON

Websites are <u>an important part of our business,</u> as they are with most any business nowadays. A lot of people will <u>go to your website </u>nowadays to check you out, to <u>see if you're real </u>before they'll even call the phone number. I find that many of my students are getting at least half their deals coming through their websites nowadays, and that number is increasing as time goes on.

Besides, think about it. If they go to your website, they don't have to talk to anybody. It's nonthreatening. They can do it at 3:00 o'clock in the morning, and then make a decision on whether they want to call you or not.

The websites are not complicated. Here's what should be on it. Number one, a homepage. The homepage is just who you are, and what you can do for them. It's the same information you have in your letter or your other marketing.

Get your U.S.P. up there. Grab their attention. Very few graphics, maybe your picture. Load it with copy, not graphics. The second thing that needs to be on there is a Property Information Sheet. In other words, are you interested in selling your home? If so, fill out this information, press send, and we'll respond to you immediately. Really that's all you need. Homepage telling them why they want to do business with you, and then a place for them to fill out the information to send it to you.

Website won't work unless people come to it. So you spend a little time learning the art of driving traffic to that website, and you'll get a lot of good deals directly from it. It's all autopilot. It comes right back to my famous saying, "The less I do, the more I make."

LYNETTE

You thinker brains can waste a whole month on this. Don't do it! Get to it! The quickest and easiest way I know is to sign up with Ron LeGrand and Global Publishing's Gold Club. Check them out at RonsGoldClub.com.

Once you get the darn thing up on the internet you can just lay back and collect the leads! If a prospect looks at your website, then types in all of their information, you know they are more serious.

You'll want to <u>advertise your web address</u> in your marketing. With the Gold Club your website is tied in with thousands of other websites, so a lot of leads come in without even advertising.

Your website is like your vehicle sign. Get it done once, <u>get it done quick</u>, and move on. The leads will take care of themselves.

Depending on how you are hooked up, you may not get a flood of leads pouring in over the internet. I've also seen a lot of good man-hours go down the drain while investors are supposedly "checking their website."

The quality sometimes depends on how they found your website in the first place. Since the prospects have already looked at your website and then decided to type in their information, they've already pre-screened themselves somewhat. There are definitely good deals floating around on the internet.

BRIAN

If you don't have a website address to give out, especially if a Seller or Buyer asks for it, it can damage your credibility. You just don't seem as professional.

When a Prospect finds your website through the address on a marketing piece, it increases response rates and reinforces your messaging. The professional appearance of your website also affects the response, as well as bolstering your credibility.

Try to pick a URL (your website address) that is easy to remember and hopefully doesn't need to be spelled out when given verbally. The only real messaging you need on your Website can be copied directly from the back of your business card. No matter what, just make a commitment right now that your website will be up in less than 2 weeks from today. Accomplish that, and then I'll know it's not holding you back like it did me. It's better to just accept that a good website is a necessary cost of doing business, like rent for a brick and mortar operation. Promote your website when and where you can, and follow up as quickly as possible on any leads because they may well be shopping around. Also, just remember that when a Prospect calls your phone you've captured their contact info, unlike a visitor to your website who may screen you out and never speak with you. What that means to you is that **your phone number should be bigger in your marketing**, you'd rather have them call than go visit your website.

My main tips in conclusion are to get your Website set up within the next 2 weeks or less, and when Leads come from your Website respond to them ASAP!

4. Roadside Signs – Bit of a Pain, Reliably Productive

RON'S KEY POINTS

I've never put out roadside signs where I didn't get calls on them. It's one of the <u>most widely used</u> <u>tools</u> in our arsenal with my students <u>nationwide</u>. By roadside signs, we mean the little 18 x 24 signs. Little fiberboard signs that you can order from sign shops, You're either going to <u>nail them up or stick them in the ground</u>, one of the two. Both of them should be done. If a sign is out on the street, it's easy to read.

<u>Big, bold, bloc k letters</u>. Nothing fancy. Do not put graphics on a sign. I would <u>make them double- sided</u>. Some students make them single-sided. The Wolffs like the double-sided. Two for one, bang for your buck I'll tell you this. They work. And, they work very well. In fact, I have students driving their entire business by doing nothing but putting out signs on a regular basis.

Should you, as the real estate entrepreneur, be the one putting out signs? The answer is no. <u>You should hire somebody</u> to put them out. A good place to get a sign distributor or distributor is the people who put them out for builders.

Anybody who puts them out for builders, they charge you about a buck or so per sign to put it out and take it down. Or just get some kid or someone who needs something to do.

You do not have to have signs out to run a very thriving business, but it is one of the things that's very inexpensive and it works better than a lot of things as far as getting sellers to call you.

I've been at this a long time. I've taught an awful lot of people how to find deals, and signs are always right near the top of that list.

LYNETTE'S KEY POINTS

For most investors, roadside signs are the most challenging marketing to distribute. Number one, you really should be getting out there at the crack of dawn every Saturday, and many of us aren't too crazy about climbing out of bed that early on the weekend.

We used to do our signs on Friday night, but we learned quickly that there were a lot more cars out there then, and it's dark. You're pulling off, parking your car, and crossing roads, so the less traffic the better.

Putting up the signs, especially if the ground is hard, is <u>no piece of cake</u>. But if you can get signs up consistently, you'll have my respect and some <u>great leads</u> too! Now remember, you can always <u>hire someone else </u>to put your signs up.

Signs get calls. It's that simple. A bunch of our first deals were from signs. As long as they're not Realtors or other Investors, these prospects are generally serious.

They saw your sign at the right place at the right time. Or they've seen your signs 2 or 3 times and they finally decided to give you a shot. There's <u>good motivation </u>in this group.

BRIAN'S KEY POINTS

First I want to point out the Messaging you'll see on our sample Roadside Signs. Often you might see a sign that says "We Buy Houses, CASH." When seeking Creative Financing Deals, you will NEVER use that word on your signs, CASH. We don't pay cash for houses, and we don't use our own credit either. That's the undeniable beauty of Creative Financing.

We like to say "Sell Now for Top Price", or other USPs you'll see on the samples to follow.

How many signs should you put out per week? Depending on your Farm Area, how spread out it is, traffic, and installation challenges, shoot for at least 20. Now 40-50 is a bigger challenge, but I will tell you that when we started out it was the only Method I felt like I could count on 100%. Therefore I was always anxious when I wasn't getting 50 signs out most every weekend.

Now I'll tell you that I would get up at 5:00 am on Saturday, grab a water bottle, and throw the signs and installation kit in the car. Depending on your procedure, your installation kit may be just signs, or it may include zip ties to put signs on poles or trees. If you live in an area with hard ground your installation kit may consist of a rubber mallet and huge screwdriver, or even a portable drill.

It's distinctly helpful if you have an accomplice, a "Wheel Man", as they say in the old heist movies. They pull up, you hop out with the sign, then they circle back around to re- acquire you. If you can work it out, it makes the job more than twice as easy, quite a bit safer, and cuts your time by 60%--70%.

You may get between a 2%, all the way up to even a 10% response. Remember Marketing Principle #4, Consistency is Crucial. Some Prospects will only respond after seeing your sign on multiple occasions. When you practice consistent placement, Signs are <u>consistent performers</u>. We all strive for that, don't we? Check out these samples.

We Buy Houses
Sell FAST for TOP Price!
YourWebsite·com
555-555-5555

This first sign is simple with good USPs that look hand-written. This font is *MV Boli* (in Word) or you can find a different font that looks handwritten if you want.

We displayed the Website on this one, which we usually don't, but so many of our students have website addresses that they're very proud of *(because we helped pick their URL)!*

Why don't we always put our website on our signs? We're concerned they'll go on their smart phone and we'll lose them forever to the Internet, whereas if they would've just called we'd have captured their phone number (even if they didn't leave a message). *One way we got 'em, the other way we didn't.*

Some Investors prefer the bold block letters, such as you see next with the **Impact Font**. You can read the sign from farther away, which is a big plus. However some Investors still like the informal "D.I.Y." look of the "handwritten" signs.

Sell Your Home Now
No Commissions, No Closing Costs, No Hassles!
555-555-5555

You can also mix and match your U.S.P.s, your Marketing Messages, but **keep your font style and colors consistent**. Most Investors believe the best sign for attracting attention and delivering the message is yellow with black letters.

Others like white with blue letters, or colored boxes with white lettering inside. Choose what you like, our students have good results with all different design schemes. Just make sure the message is legible, and consistently delivered into the same Farm Areas.

Remember Marketing Principle #4, Consistency is Crucial.

If you change up your sign design every week your local customers won't know it's always you out there with the signs. Consistent sign placement truly builds credibility over time. Maintaining your same sign appearance builds your brand and **overall** presence in your Farm Areas.

5. Outbound Calls – Mandatory for Beginners, Call Zillow, Craigslist, other FSBO Leads

RON'S KEY POINTS

The deal is that I want you to call all of these ads, and fill out a property information sheet. I want you to get the answers to these questions. Remember, these people are advertising. They expect someone to call, so it's not like you're interrupting their dinner. Or of course you can find someone who likes talking on the telephone and is a good communicator.

Sometimes you'll have another person calling on ads, and this person is filling out the property information sheet. They're disclosing clearly that they're getting some information for their boss, who will be in touch with them after they get it.

I want you to certainly call all the FSBO ads. Just for sale by owner. You may have anywhere from 10-15 calls to 100 calls. I would suggest that you call them at night from 6:00-9:00 pm, because that's when people are home. That's when you're going to get a hold of them.

Call until you exhaust all that list, and if they can't reach them then they can try during the day. Maybe on Monday during the day. Call until you reach all of them you're going to reach. Believe it or not, you won't reach them all, because some people just aren't reachable. You know, it kills me. They run an ad and they're never around to answer the phone. And you wonder why houses don't get sold. It's usually because of the person in charge of making the sale.

Let them leave a message, and also have them call back. It's a numbers game. Again, a key point—If you're going to do this from your home, it ain't going to work. It ain't going to work, because you're going to find something better to do and you're going to find some reason not to do it.

The only way it's going to work is if you pay somebody, and make it their responsibility to deliver those leads to you. If they don't, you fire them and get somebody else. If you do that every week, you probably don't need to do anything else.

You can also call on the "Houses For Rent" section as well, because many landlords are motivated sellers. They got this house, they put a tenant in it, and they have no clue what they're doing.

They've never taken the time to learn landlording. They figured maybe it just comes from God or something, and here they are with these tenants who are causing grief in their life.

Now you let them know that you're interested in buying houses, and sure enough you will be buying some from the "For Rent" section. That's a good tip.

Remember, they're not getting calls from investors like you. They're getting calls from more bad tenants. Most landlords who are advertising for renters in the paper have a miserable life. So you come along and put a little sunshine back in their life.

LYNETTE'S KEY POINTS

Call from websites or jot down any numbers you see on signs. Then start calling all the "For Sale By Owners" and the "Houses For Rent" you can find.

It's usually better to have prospects calling you than vice versa. You will have to <u>weed through </u>some unmotivated, annoying sellers.

You don't have to wait around for the phone to ring. Plus this <u>builds your mental toughness</u>. It's good for you. Now we do say that if you start feeling discouraged, stop. Remember what Ron talks about. You can just find someone with a big mouth, and <u>pay them to call for you</u>.

You're usually not going to convert a high percentage of these, and a seller or two might get grouchy with you. That's okay. You need some "crazy seller" stories to tell on your yacht.

BRIAN'S KEY POINTS

Outbound Calls are also referred to as FSBO Calls. That stands for "For Sale By Owner". It means Opening Calls are being made to Sellers who have personally advertised their home for sale. These Sellers have not listed their home with a Realtor, they've decided to try to sell it themselves. That makes them prime candidates for us for many reasons.

Now usually we like it better when the Seller calls us. When do you think the Seller is more motivated and you're in a better bargaining position, when you call them or when they call you? When they call you, of course.

However, with Outbound Calls you don't have to wait for a response to some Marketing Message you have out there. You can take the initiative and make the contact yourself, therefore you can turn this Method on and off easily. You should pretty much always have it on. You can make these Outbound Calls yourself, or you can delegate them.

Outbound Calls to sources such as Zillow, Craigslist, and other FSBO Webstes can be <u>a bonanza</u>. The most challenging part of getting started doing outbound calls, is that you've got to be a little mentally tough to pick up that phone. Either that or delegate to a Virtual Assistant or a local FSBO Caller or Acquisitionist. It's not so tough when you've got the whole script right in front of you. It's actually good for you to just start calling and use the script. It's good experience to call these leads in the beginning.

You need to fight through some unmotivated sellers, or have your person do it. <u>It's all a numbers game</u>. If you're calling these leas consistently, you're going to get deals. **So keep on plugging away!**

Date_____   **FSBO Call Script**   Source_____

Hi, I'm calling about buying your house, is it still for sale?_____ Great, I'm _____, and what's your name?

Owner(s)_____ (fill in [ ] info from the FSBO Ad)

[Phone_____ Address_____]

So I see your asking price is ___, is that right? _____ (MY COMPS_____)

BR/BA_____ SQ FT_____ What kind of shape is property in, need repairs?_____

So are you living in the house right now? _____ Can I ask **why you're selling**?_____

Okay, we're definitely interested in buying your house. You know, a lot of times it works out best by doing something with the financing. So do you own the house free and clear, or do you have a mortgage on it?

F&C   Mtg   (IF **F & C**, GO TO BOX **2**.) (IF **Mortgage**:) And approximately how much is owed on that?

1st $_____ Payment PITI_____	Current? YES NO	(How late?)_____
2nd $_____ Payment PITI_____	Current? YES NO	(How late?)_____

1. Owe 85-90%+ of House Value (% depends on market) ➤ Let me ask you, would you sell us the house for what you owe on it?   YES   NO

If YES, Go to*** below. If NO, continue:

Okay, well if we were to work it out and close whenever you want, what's the least you would take?_____ Is that the best you can do?_____

Great, well we work with houses like yours a lot.

Down Pymt: $_____   Monthly: _____   Term_____   DOM__ | Now the way it normally works is that we buy the house from you with owner financing or lease purchase, and we make monthly payments. A few great things about how we do it are that we pay a good price, we can close whenever you want, and we take care of everything, so you're free and you can just move on.

Doesn't that sound good/great?   YES   NO

2. Mortgaged House OR Free & Clear ➤ Great, well we work with houses like yours a lot. Now the way it normally works is that we buy the house from you with owner financing or lease purchase, and we make monthly payments. A few great things about how we do it are that we pay a good price, we can close whenever you want, and we take care of everything, so you're free and you can just move on.

Doesn't that sound good/great?   YES   NO

If YES: Okay, so when it comes to purchase price, if we work everything out and close whenever you want, what's the least you would take? _____

Is that the best you can do?_____ (GO TO ***)

If NO: Okay, sometimes people do need all their cash out right away. We usually buy from sellers who want to make more money from the sale, and can wait a little while to cash out. Is that possible, could you maybe give us a little time to pay you off in full?

YES   MAYBE   NO

IF YES: ***What's the best time my boss/partner/I could call you back? (or start **Closing Call**)_____

IF NO/MAYBE or REQUESTING MORE INFORMATION, put lead in Follow-up File or Suspect File.

Just a couple last things now, is the house LISTED? YES NO | Is it **Vacant / Rented / You Live In It?**

Notes/Follow-up_____

Okay, great, it's been a pleasure talking with you. I really think this will work out good/great for you, and good for us too. We're looking forward to talking with you again   later today / tomorrow / soon!   –TheWolffCouple.com

Now we've covered **the first 5** of the *14 Main Marketing Methods*. These are the most important ones to focus on at the start, so we're not going to confuse you by delving into all the other Methods. If you want further training on ALL the Marketing Methods, complete with digital samples, call us at 888-Rich-Now and ask about our **Wolff-LeGrand "Masterful Marketing" System.**

RON'S KEY POINTS

What I love about Marketing is that it **generates a lot of revenue** if you do it correctly. We all love revenue! You no longer have any excuses why your **phone isn't ringing at least 20- 30 times** per month! When you do as we teach here, you're sure to have some impressive success stories. Don't forget to send them to the Wolffs and me!

BRIAN

We are so glad you got this amazing and comprehensive book. Now follow the Marketing training here, choose **3 to 5** Methods to start with, and **Take Action** immediately!

Our goal with this book is nothing less than **changing your life**. I hope you learned **Facts** here that, when you apply them, will forever change your life for the better.

Get leads pouring in, and everything else will take care of itself! We can't wait to hear from you with a great testimonial letter!

LYNETTE

We want to thank Ron for joining us here on the all-important topic of Marketing, he is filled with incredible money-making wisdom. Ron has been a wonderful mentor and friend to both of us.

In closing, I just want to say to you that opportunity is knocking. In your hands right now is everything you need to open the door to an amazing new life -- The Life of Your Dreams.

All you have to do now is...*TAKE ACTION!*

Chapter 5
What You **Say** Determines What You **Make**

From the moment sellers pick up the phone, all they are judging you by is **what you say and how you say it.** We believe 2 things about this business -- first, **the most important part of every deal is the Closing Call.**

Second, that automatically means **the most important tools in the entire business are Scripts**.

For over 15 years we've been going up on stage in front of hundreds of students, with *their* leads, and doing **LIVE Closing Calls to real sellers**. I am proud to say that we let the student keep all the profits, and we've made them millions of dollars over all these years!

You've read some of their testimonials already. We want you to have a testimonial letter just like these. Your best chance, and the biggest single piece of advice we give to our students is…

STICK TO THE SCRIPT!

We only say this because we really really want you to close a deal, and the biggest obstacle is **foot-in-mouth disease.** But we know you won't say the wrong thing (or anything stupid that blows the deal) if you just say what's written in the scripts.

We have some really powerful scripts coming up in this chapter, real scripts that you will use to close deals. Remember, **I wrote screenplays in Hollywood for** 7 years -- these scripts are amazingly **smooth, conversational,** and **user-friendly.**

This is mostly a phone job, so **the sellers and buyers can't see you reading your scripts**. Just make sure you **have them handy** every time you get on the phone with prospects.

Phil & Cindy Salazar - *Tacoma, WA*

What can we say…. **Scripts, scripts, scripts!!** We love them, and we don't know what we'd do without them! We can honestly say the reason we chose the Wolffs was their scripts, especially after we watched Brian & Lynette in action on the phone <u>reading their own scripts live</u> with sellers!

The scripts are the reason we just closed our first deal. Yessss!! We can truly say with a whole heart, how incredibly VALUABLE YOUR MOTIVATION, FAITH IN US & AUDACITY IN MAKING US STAY THE COURSE has been. --Thank you, thank you, thank you! Our shut up check is: $12,000.00 with a monthly cash flow of $350/mo for the next 5 yrs = $43,000 Profit on this one deal!

We depend on the scripts so much we keep them accessible at all times. When you just follow the scripts, you get and give all the info to make it a successful call.

It is much easier to not forget anything if you have a script to read because they are concise, clear, non- intimidating, matter-of-fact explanations of the solutions we offer.

It also helps to keep things to-the-point and not waste time or "paint yourself into a corner" by bringing up things that could create confusion or more questions.

Scripts give you the confidence to make the call! When it was my turn (Cindy) to make the calls, there was no way I would pick up the phone without the scripts in front of me. We closed another deal and got an $80,000 Down Payment, with a $600 monthly cash flow!

Wooo Hooo... Screamin' Deals!! Thank you, Brian & Lynette Wolff!

Jamie Parker - *Los Angeles, CA*

I just wanted to let everyone know what the Wolffs have done for me. With their help and scripts, within 60 days I had done my first 8 deals!

The proof is in what they are teaching you. In one month I made over $68,000 from 3 separate deals. I've done many deals now of all kinds. The future of my family, my beautiful wife and baby, has changed forever. The Wolff Couple have been so instrumental in my success and motivation!

Thank you Brian & Lynette!

If you don't stick to the scripts, even if you're feeling extra confident, **you will get lost**. I have listened to recordings of our students, and when they go off script many times they think they're saying something clever, but in reality they're either **alienating or confusing the seller**. Unless you've really done this Creative Financing stuff for a while and you really know what you're doing, you probably don't know what you're doing. Let us guide you, **stick to what we teach, and you'll be okay**.

So reading a script into the phone, setting up an appointment, going to meet a prospect at their house…this sounds suspiciously like a sales job.

Real Estate Investing does have a **sales component**, as well as many other Action Steps. When you're talking to sellers and buyers, however you want to frame it, it is sales. Hey, you sell yourself every time you walk into a room and meet someone new. And what you're selling here is a strong plan or **strategy to solve their house problem**. Don't be worried if you've never had any sales experience or you don't think of yourself as a salesperson.

Here's how we think about it - **The Closing Process** is, at its core, **making a series of decisions**. The seller and you must agree on these decisions, and **write them down in an agreement**. That's how you buy a house, that's how you sell a house. You guide the seller, and then the buyer, through the "Sales Process" of making these decisions. In essence, you are a **shepherd**, guiding your customers through an often difficult trek. You're there to help them make all the right decisions, and help make all those decisions easier, If they **make one wrong decision** along the way, the whole sales process could be thrown off and **the deal lost forever**.

There are plenty of smaller decisions the seller has to make, and there are **4 Big Decisions**. When you buy an ugly house from a bank, there is only 1 deal point – purchase price. But when we work out Creative

Financing deals with sellers, there are 4 main deal points that we **MUST agree on** for the deal to move forward.

4 Creative Financing Deal Points:

1. Purchase Price
2. Monthly Payment
3. Length of Term
4. Down Payment/Option Deposit

Those are the **Big 4**, if you can get those worked out then you should have a deal! If you can't get to mutually acceptable Terms, however, then nobody can write something in a blank space on the agreement. If every one of those 4 spaces aren't filled in, **there is no deal**.

Sometimes you may not realize **how stressful this can be** for a seller, making all these decisions. If you get a seller who is not good at making decisions, good luck. It'll be a long Deal Meeting, if you ever even get there. But even if you have a **very wayward sheep**, you continue to play the **"Good Shepherd Investor",** and keep patiently trying to guide them through to the end of the sales process.

So let's examine some of the big and little decisions the seller has to make with you. Of course you are the Good Shepherd Investor guiding them through this challenging decision-making process.

Seller Decision Series

Overall Decision:

Am I selling my house to this investor?

Specific Decisions:

PHONE RINGS

What's the Caller ID? Don't recognize it, it's about the house.

Do I have time to talk to someone right now about my house?

Do I feel like talking to someone right now about my house?

DECIDE to PICK UP

Do I like the sound of this person's voice?

Can I understand what they're saying?

Do they seem professional? Are they just another Realtor?

How do I feel about Investors?

Is this person friendly?

Does this person care about what I want or need?

Do I want to keep talking to this person?

Can I trust this person?

Is this a scam?

Does it sound like an attractive deal?

What would I get out of this? Should I answer their questions?

DECIDE to PROCEED

Why do they want time to pay me off in full?

Could I give them a little time to pay me off in full?

How long could I give them?

How much will I sell the house for?

How much do I want for a monthly payment?

Do I need or want a down payment?

How much down payment do I need?

When can I meet with this investor?

Are the terms we discussed acceptable to me?

When do I want to close? When am I moving out?

Where am I moving to?

Needless to say, **this is a lot of __decisions__**. THEY NEED HELP! That's why you're there, to shepherd them through the sometimes **scary 4 Step Process** below. They want to sell their house to you, but they're also be **terrified of making a big mistake**. Tricky decisions are sometimes part of the house- selling process, so use scripts to **shepherd scared seller-sheep** through these 4 Steps!

4 Steps of the Closing Process

1. Make Friends
2. Present the Benefits
3. Decide on Terms
4. Ask for the Sale

These apply to ALL Creative Financing Deals.

When we started at this business we'd both had lots of sales experience, we knew the 4 Steps. We knew to be the best closers, we needed to **follow this tried-and-true 4-step process.**

This is true whenever you're selling a *big ticket item* that *requires explanation* and some level of *negotiation*. It was true when I sold encyclopedias door-to-door, when I sold cars, houses, even luxury vacuum cleaners! Let's look at the best ways to **use these Steps as stepping stones** to huge paychecks!

1. Make Friends

First and foremost, your prospects **must trust you**. After all, they are **entrusting their house** and their **credit** and certainly their **peace of mind** with you. The easiest way to build trust is to *"Make Friends"*. People trust people who they like. You can't begin to calculate how much it pays off when you take just 30-60 seconds to **Build Rapport!**

After building Rapport everything **flows so much easier**, even getting mortgage information. You've taken away any adversarial stance, you've put yourself on the same side of the fence as your prospect. Now you're **working together** to solve your new friend and prospect's house challenge! Building Rapport even makes your customers more fun!

Everyone wants to work with friendly and knowledgeable people. Even if you're not so knowledgeable, your prospects **will be very forgiving** when they like you. Your posture should be open and friendly. Let them know who you are and what you do.

You can use this "Nice Neighbor" Script early in the conversation if the prospect is showing signs of hesitation, especially if they refuse to give mortgage information. You don't need to say the whole script or say it verbatim, just get the main points across in a **relaxed and friendly** manner.

"NICE NEIGHBORS" RAPPORT-BUILDING SCRIPT

Now just so you'll know a little bit about us, we're local here, we work with folks all around the area. We live here and we work here, and we use a few different ways to buy and sell houses here. Sometimes we fix up houses, or help families get into nice houses. Now when we buy a distressed house we usually pay cash.

With a nicer (higher quality) house like yours we would buy it using Owner Financing or a Lease Purchase. That just means that you give us a little time to pay you off in full. Do you think that might work out for you guys?

A lot of times we can buy the house fast and easy by doing something with the financing. Now most of the people whose houses we buy, they have one or two mortgages. So do you have a mortgage on the house, or is it free and clear?

(If "Free & Clear", go on. IF <u>Mortgage</u>:)
And approximately how much is owed on that?"
(continue Closing Call)

This script is good for relaxing your prospect, building trust, and giving them enough comfort to want to proceed.

You'll notice our scripts are very conversational, with plenty of words like "sure, so, okay." It so happens that for 7 years we lived in Hollywood, and I wrote over 20 feature movie scripts and about a dozen TV episodes.

I didn't get rich and famous, but **I got really good at writing scripts** the way normal people talk. So that turned out good for <u>*you*</u> now! You always want to sound as natural and real as possible to connect with people and be the most effective closer.

We talk about Building Rapport everywhere we go, but didn't we all learn about making friends in kindergarten? Maybe we did, but instantly sliding into an easy-going Rapport with a customer is a **true skill** and a gift. Fortunately it's a skill that **can be taught**, and it's as easy as **learning a few scripts**.

Sometimes hardened, war-torn Rehabbers resist us when we push this *Making Friends* thing. We smile, but let's actually make a **rational case** for the value of Making Friends/Building Rapport. There are a couple simple truths that apply, which we ignore to our own detriment.

THE LOGICAL ARGUMENT
FOR MAKING FRIENDS

Premise 1: People tend to trust people they like.
Premise 2: The easiest way to get people to like you is be friendly to them
Premise 3: To get deals, Investors need people to trust them.

Conclusion: Investors need to be friendly to get deals.

Do you think we're overstating the argument? We're not. Some Investors are *all business*, they ignore the value of "chatting up" the sellers and buyers. They know little to nothing about their customers personally, and there is no emotional bond between them. **That ain't us!** If you **want more business**, that shouldn't be you either.

Your customers are going through a life transition, it's naturally a very emotional time. They are often open to you reaching out beyond just the "stats" on the house.

We've seen countless houses and talked with countless sellers and buyers, and there is one truth for sure.

**Real Estate Investing is much easier
and more fun when everyone's friendly.**

We can't begin to describe the power of taking a few moments at the outset of the process to get to know who you are talking to (and hopefully working with). Most of your customers, even supposedly hard-bitten investors, will loosen up and be more flexible when you've taken the time to **Make Friends!**

**Here's some powerful scripts to ensure
you'll build great rapport, and reap the rewards!**

Rapport Building Scripts

1. **House** What can you tell me about the house? When was it built? What do you like best about it? Any special home improvements or landscaping? Nice!

2. **Kids** How many kids do you have? I love kids. How old are they? That's such a (cute/fun/tricky) age.
    My kid/niece/neighbor is (age).
    TIP: Always relate kid questions to your kids/grandkids/kids you know

3. **Pets** I hear you have a dog/cat/bird/etc. What kind do you have? That's one of my favorite kinds. I used to have a (breed/type). Such a great pet.

4. **Neighborhood** How is your neighborhood there? Are there a lot of kids? Any parks or anything close that you can walk to? Are you pretty close to the freeway? Did you grow up around there?

5. **Area or State** How long have you lived in…? Where are you from originally? I love that state, I have some relatives/friends that live there.
    TIP: Geographic rapport-building always seems to work.

6. **Local Teams** Did you catch the (team)'s game last night? Some game, huh? And how about (top player)? What a game he/she had. I'm a huge fan. or I'm really more of a (team)'s fan.
    TIP: Usually works better with men. Duh.

7. **Health** I'm sorry you're not feeling well. My mom/dad/grandma/etc had that same exact thing. It is rough.

TIP: Don't bring up health unless they do, then show lots of compassion (we all want that when we're sick).

8. **Weather** This weather we've been having is crazy. It's been so wet/dry/hot/cold. I need a vacation away from it. Maybe it's that global warming.

9. **Time of Week** T.G.I.F.! / I hate Mondays, don't you? I love the weekend! / We made it to hump day!

10. **Holidays** Did you have a nice...? / Are you doing anything special for... Christmas / 4th of July / Valentine's Day / etc.? We're planning to...

11. **Work** What kind of work do you do? Hey, my dad/friend/brother is in that field. I've heard things are going well/not so well. How long have you done that? I've always been interested in that. It must be interesting work. Do you like it?

12. **Marriage** How long have you two been married? Wow. I bet it feels like you're still on your honeymoon, right? *(not for use on divorce deals)*
    My husband/wife and I have been married ___ years. It just keeps getting better and better!

2. Present the Benefits

Whatever Benefits the seller sees in the deal, whatever their *hot buttons* are (like "Instant Sale" or "No Commissions" or "We Buy As-Is"), you keep pushing those hot buttons. That's called Presenting *(or Pushing)* the Benefits!.

This is the time for you to get enthusiastic about the Benefits, and **how they'll help your prospect**. We are obviously huge believers in enthusiasm -- you already know that famous author Dan Kennedy gave us our nickname, *Mr. and Mrs. Enthusiasm!*

Always remember that **"Enthusiasm is Contagious!"** Here are some "hot buttons" for you to push with sellers on Closing Calls and in Deal Meetings.

Benefits to Seller
(Presented Enthusiastically)

➤ Instant Sale -- You can move on with your life!

➤ Debt Relief -- No more making those payments!

➤ Freedom -- Not chained to that house anymore!

➤ No Commissions, No Closing Costs! – Save $!

➤ Don't have to talk to a bunch of Realtors!

➤ Don't have to fix house, we buy "As-is"!!

➤ Don't have a lot of people going through house!

➤ Don't have to worry about if house will sell!

➤ Easy Sale, No Complicated Paperwork!

If your prospect is at all flexible, seek out which of these benefits **mean the most to them**. Then keep pushing those hot buttons with enthusiasm until you come to the Key Step #3, "Decide on Terms"

3. Decide on Terms

We've covered the **4 Creative Financing** (or *Pretty House*) **Deal Points,** but we want to keep repeating them until they become totally second nature to you:

1. Purchase Price
2. Monthly Payment
3. Length of Term
4. Down Payment/Option Deposit

Until these **4 Terms** are decided upon and written into the agreement, you should **always be closing**. This may sound **pressure-filled** and scary, but it isn't because you have the **perfect road map** to follow in the <u>SCRIPTS</u>. Get on the phone or in person with the seller, and say **the exact lines** we gave you. You'll be amazed at how our "Magic Words Work! **A.B.C. – "Always Be Closing!"**

4. Ask for the Sale

The first 3 Steps **don't amount to a thing** if you don't **Ask for the Sale**, and end up with a signed contract that leads to a big check.

This is when a lot of people fall apart, honestly, because they just **chicken out at the end** and they can't quite punch that football into the end zone *(excuse the mixed metaphors)*. Our System takes you from the start of "Making Friends" on the **Opening Call**, all the way to "Asking for the Sale" at the **Deal Meeting**. With all that training, you'll be so prepared you won't be afraid!

You can't get the signed contract over the phone. On the **Closing Call, "Asking for the Sale" means Setting the Appointment.** That means when you hang up you want to have a time to go see the house and the seller.

We have a perfect script for this, and the key is the sooner the better. That means **today if possible**, a sense of **urgency is vital**. When you have a meeting of the minds on the phone, and **mostly agree on the 4 Deal Points**, then just set a time! Then you type up your agreements, and get your butt out to the house!

At the **Deal Meeting, "Asking for the Sale"** means **finalizing the 4 Deal Points**, and requesting the **seller's signature** on the bottom line!

After you sign the paperwork you're on your way, you're going to make some **big money**. We want to get you to the point of *"Asking for the Sale"* on every deal possible!

Get that signature, get that deal, cash that check!

As Lynette loves to say, **"Cha-ching, cha-ching!"**

To be the **most effective Closer**, just stay focused on

4 Steps of the Closing Process

1. Make Friends
2. Present the Benefits
3. Decide on Terms
4. Ask for the Sale!

Creative Financing Deal Overview

It's important to understand the **Steps of every Creative Financing Deal**. Essentially it all begins with **Marketing**, which connects you with your Prospect in one way or another. Then we move into the **money-making steps** you see in the flow diagram below.

3 Steps to Every Deal

1. **Opening Call**
2. **Closing Call**
3. **Deal Meeting**

1. Opening Call

The first step in the interaction process with the sellers is the Opening Call. The form to use is the **FSBO Call Script.**

3 Goals of the Opening Call:

> **Establish Credibility** – _professionalism & investing knowledge_
> **Build Rapport** – _making friends and influencing people!_
> **Gather Information**
>> ✓ Basic Facts – _bedrooms, bathrooms, sq footage, repairs, year built, Days On Market, who is living in home_
>> ✓ Why & When Seller is Moving – _shows motivation level_
>> ✓ Mortgage Information – _usually most challenging to get_
>> ✓ Seller Flexibility – _can they give us time to pay in full?_

Many of the properties you or your staff will be calling on will be listed on Zillow, Craigslist, or another internet site.

That's probably where you got the phone number or email in the first place, actually. Since that's the case, just take the basic information (bedrooms, bathrooms, square footage, etc.) directly from the posting. Otherwise you only waste the seller's time and your own, not to mention annoying the seller when you want to be ingratiating yourself.

This Opening Call is your chance to practice your **Rapport- building skills.** Remember to use your own **Real Estate Investor Bio** as well, this can relax the customer because it lets them know who they're talking to, not just some voice on the phone grilling them. When you write an effective REI Bio, it is the gift that keeps on giving every call.

Before you say your Bio the seller often seems a little wary, **unsure about you** and what this is all about. Then about 20 seconds later you can practically hear the relief and the smile come to the seller's face, "Oh, you're like a **friendly neighbor who buys and sells houses** and likes to help folks out. I thought you were some kind of hedge fund cutthroat or something, what do I know?"

Now don't force your Bio in prematurely and awkwardly. A big reason it is effective is it seems natural and neighborly, not forced. Here's more detail on crafting and using your own.

YOUR REAL ESTATE INVESTOR BIOGRAPHY

Your **REI Bio** is simply a 2-5 sentence explanation of who you are. Your goal for your Bio is to Build trust in **4 Ways**:

1. Demonstrate Stability through Ties to the Area
2. Show Credibility and/or a Trustworthy Nature
3. Display Real Estate Credibility
4. Be Friendly and Neighborly

Now you don't launch into your REI Bio at the very start of the Opening or Closing Call. This should come after sharing pleasantries and perhaps confirming a few facts about the house. You'll usually get optimum impact when it's prior to discussing your offer, or any of the **4 Deal Points** (1. Purchase Price, 2. Monthly Payment, 3. Length of Term, 4. Down Payment/Option Deposit).

The first line of your REI Bio should be about **your ties to the area**, especially when related to the house location.

Next **mention your regular job in a positive light**, especially when it makes you seem particularly **nice or credible**. Jobs like teacher or nurse sound nice, pilot or engineer sound credible, or you can always just mention where you work or **what field you're in**.

You follow that up with **your real estate credibility**. It's good if you have some, if not you can always calculate from when you bought your first house, and say "I've been involved in Real Estate for 20 years."

This next credibility line can sometimes work well, and sometimes it raises more questions than it answers: "I'm with a group that has been doing these kinds of deals all across the country for over 30 years." You're in with Ron LeGrand and us, so that is true! Just be careful how you use it, only if really needed, but you should usually have something better to rely on in your own Bio.

Finish with a line that makes you seem **nice and neighborly**, like how you really like working with sellers and buyers in the area. Here's a sample REI Bio from one of our characters, the Wholesale Buyer in our "What to Say" System:

"Hi, I'm Jerome Nutley, I've lived here for over 10 years/my whole life, just a few miles from your house actually. I've been an engineer at the Honeywell plant over there on Main Street for a long time, and I also buy and sell houses all around our area. I really like working with sellers here in our area, we can usually work out really great win-win deals."

Your Bio will follow this general guide and should usually be **15-30 seconds**, unless you have something really special to mention that you think wil make a big positive impact. You can follow up your Bio with a line like, "Now after looking at the house and the numbers, here's how we would buy it."

Then just go into the rest of the Closing Call, with the goals of working out the 4 Deal Points (see previous list), and setting an appointment for a Deal Meeting. Also don't neglect to use our 33 Top Negotiating Techniques for Investing, which we teach at our "Changing Your Life" Workshop!

So that is our quick guide for creating and using **your own REI Bio, Real Estate Investor Biography, your story!**

Here's the script that we and our students use for Opening Calls, the FSBO Call Script. The most challenging information to get from a seller is usually what they owe on their mortgage. See how we **effectively anticipate that objection**, and defuse it to get the info.

OPENING CALL SCRIPT

Date_____ **FSBO Call Script** Source _____

Hi, I'm calling about buying your house, is it still for sale?_____ Great, I'm _____, and what's your name?

Owner(s)_____ *(fill in [ ] info from the FSBO Ad)*

[Phone_____ Address_____]

So I see your asking price is ___, is that right? _____ *(MY COMPS_____)*

BR/BA_____ SQ FT_____ What kind of shape is property in, need repairs?_____

So are you living in the house right now? _____ Can I ask **why you're selling**?_____

Okay, we're definitely interested in buying your house. You know, a lot of times it works out best by doing something with the financing. So do you own the house free and clear, or do you have a mortgage on it?
F&C Mtg (IF **F & C**, GO TO BOX **2**.) (IF **Mortgage**:) And approximately how much is owed on that?

| 1st $_____ Payment PITI_____ | Current? YES NO (How late?)____ |
| 2nd $_____ Payment PITI_____ | Current? YES NO (How late?)____ |

1. Owe 85-90%+ of House Value *(% depends on market)* → Let me ask you, would you sell us the house for what you owe on it? YES NO

If YES, Go to*** below. If NO, continue:

Okay, well if we were to work it out and close whenever you want, what's the least you would take?_____ Is that the best you can do?_____

Great, well we work with houses like yours a lot.

Down Pymt: $ ____	Now the way it normally works is that we buy the house from you with owner financing or lease purchase, and we make monthly payments. A few great things about how we do it are that we pay a good price, we can close whenever you want, and we take care of everything, so you're free and you can just move on.
Monthly: ____	
Term ____	
DOM__	

Doesn't that sound good/great? YES NO

2. Mortgaged House OR Free & Clear → Great, well we work with houses like yours a lot. Now the way it normally works is that we buy the house from you with owner financing or lease purchase, and we make monthly payments. A few great things about how we do it are that we pay a good price, we can close whenever you want, and we take care of everything, so you're free and you can just move on.

Doesn't that sound good/great? YES NO

If YES: Okay, so when it comes to purchase price, if we work everything out and close whenever you want, what's the least you would take? _____
. Is that the best you can do?_____ (GO TO ***)

If NO: Okay, sometimes people do need all their cash out right away. We usually buy from sellers who want to make more money from the sale, and can wait a little while to cash out. Is that possible, could you maybe give us a little time to pay you off in full?

YES MAYBE NO

IF YES: ***What's the best time my boss/partner/I could call you back? *(or start **Closing Call**)*____
IF NO/MAYBE or *REQUESTING MORE INFORMATION*, put lead in Follow-up File or Suspect File.
Just a couple last things now, is the house LISTED? YES NO Is it Vacant / Rented / You Live In It?
Notes/Follow-up_____

Okay, great, it's been a pleasure talking with you. I really think this will work out good/great for you, and good for us too.
We're looking forward to talking with you again later today / tomorrow / soon! --*TheWolffCouple.com*

2. Closing Call

In the Creative Financing world there is **one Action Step** that can make you more in **15 minutes** than most people make in a month (or even a year)! What simple yet massively rewarding task are you performing in this crucial 15 minutes? What easily learned task can pay you off at a rate of literally **tens of thousands of dollars per hour?**

Making Closing Calls! When you know the secrets of making powerful Closing Calls, you have **the keys to the kingdom**. The Closing Call is the **Moment of Truth** when you discover if you have a suspect, or a big money prospect. It's the moment when you either **close the deal, or blow the deal.**

How you talk to your prospects, **what you say and how you say it will either make or break each deal**. It will make the difference whether you walk away with **nothing or a huge payday**. That is why the Closing Call makes some beginning investors feel anywhere from anxious to apoplectic.

Over the past 15 years we've gotten to be drop-dead amazing at making Closing Calls on Creative Financing deals. We have a reputation as being **the best in the nation** at closing deals on the phone with no money down and no credit required. Many weekends you'll find us up on stage in front of anywhere from fifty to hundreds of investing students, all hanging on every word as we close **real *Live* deals** right before their eyes! The great thing is that **we make money for the students** who bring in the leads, and we don't take a penny—we just want to see our students make huge profits! You can watch these killer videos for yourself on our channel at YouTube.com/WolffCouple.

Closing deals started for me back in college when I got a job telemarketing for Time-Life Books, and went all the way through being a Realtor and a Mortgage Broker and even managing an office for Ameriquest Mortgage. Lynette had also been a Realtor, and even set an Arizona record in New Home Sales when **she sold 41 homes in one month!**

Then we found the amazing and lucrative world of Creative Real Estate Investing through the down-to-earth guru Ron LeGrand. We left behind two 6-figure incomes and never looked back. Instead of working 50+ hours per week, now we make over twice as much money in less than 5 hours per week! It's the magic of Automation and Delegation!

<u>Steps of the Closing Call</u>

1. Get Your Seller or Buyer on the Phone
   - Best calling times – usually evenings, but vary
   - Cell phones – can reach almost anytime, but…
   - Ask "Do you have a couple minutes to talk?"
   - Talk to the Decision Maker

2. Build Rapport
   - Use Real Estate Investor Bio – *15-30 seconds*
   - First Impressions make or break deals
   - Everything goes so much smoother, so much easier to get information
   - People trust people they like
   - It makes your job more fun and rewarding —Techniques for Building Rapport
     o Mirroring Understanding & Urgency, *double U's*
     o Empathize w/ their situation, tell related story about you
     o Get them talking with the Rapport-Building Scripts —Favorite Rapport-Building Topics
       1. Their House
       2. Kids
       3. Pets

    4. Neighborhood

    5. Overall Area/State

    6. Local Teams

    7. Health

    8. Weather

    9. Time of Week

    10. Holidays

    11. Work

    12. Marriage

3. Verify Information

- House details, and "backs to"
- House condition and upgrades
- Mortgage information
- Reason for moving
- Numbers of the deal

4. Close the Deal

- Explain How Deal Works
- Get Answers on 4 Deal Points.
- Answer Questions and Objections
- Walk them through the Process
- Give follow-up Information

5. Set the Appointment

- Schedule for ASAP
- Offer choice of times

6. Sign Off (and On) with Enthusiasm

- Don't rehash deal numbers
- Set Expectations
- Say how great this'll work out for everyone
- Give Congratulations!

Let's go through these individual steps in more detail.

Get Your Seller (or Buyer) **on the Phone.** The best calling times are usually in the evening, but nowadays with cell phones you can pretty much call people anytime. When you call someone on their cell phone you don't know what their situation is, so always ask, **"Do you have a couple of minutes to talk right now?"** Always talk to the **decision-maker.** They will generally guide you to who that is, but usually it's best to get everyone on the phone who's on the deed (maybe other "influencers" too).

Build Rapport. Why build Rapport? Because first impressions make or break deals. Everything goes so much smoother when you've **"Made Friends"**, it's so **much easier to get all the information you need.**

People trust people they like. If the seller is going to sell you their home and leave the mortgage in their name, **do they have to trust you? Absolutely.**

Plus when you "make friends" with sellers your job becomes **more fun and rewarding**. Knowing people's stories it's even **more meaningful** when you help them with a home. Many of our students have made **long-time friends** with home-selling customers of the past.

One technique we like for building Rapport is "Mirroring", and there's 2 "U's" for each prospect— Understanding and Urgency. How much Understanding do they have about the deal you're offering them? You have to **talk to them on their level**. For instance, if they don't understand **"Lease Purchase"**, you might use the phrase **"Rent-to-Own"**. You're aiming for clarity, so Mirror their level of Understanding with your termin- ology and pace.

Urgency is the second **U**, so you want to determine **how fast they need to sell**, and how fast they like to do things generally. Watch how fast they talk. Ask them about their plans, and time frame. Their level of Urgency will often be revealed by their answers to the 2 questions, **"When do you want to move?"**, and **"Can I ask why you're moving?"** So you need to **Mirror their level of Urgency** as well.

You want to **empathize with their situation**. Many folks who are going through a house sale have plenty of troubles, minor and major. They're going through a big transition, and **you are there to help.** That's your goal, to be of service and shepherd them over a rocky path.

> ## *People don't care how much you know until they know how much you care.*

It's often productive to get customers talking about themselves using our **Rapport Building Scripts**. Let's touch on some of our favorite Rapport-Building topics.

Number one is their house. **"What can you tell me about the house?"** That's a favorite and logical line to get them talking. Next comes their kids, pets, and the neighborhood, which can be useful info. The overall state of the area, maybe you're both from there, maybe you've been there, moved there or whatever. Local sports team, that's always a good one with some guys.

Talking about health with elderly folks can be bonding. Nobody usually wants to hear their littanty of aches and pains, so if you show a little sympathy it can go a long way (you may just make a devoted friend quickly). Weather, you can always talk about that. The time of week, "Oh, it's TGIF," hump day, weekend, etc. If you're near a holiday that can break the ice, but careful about religious holidays. Work, whatever their job is, and only what they're open to sharing on that. Being married, that can be something that folks like to talk about, especially milestones like being married for 40 or 50 years.

Verify Information. Make sure you know some detail on the house, **anything special** about it, what's around it. Pull all the factual info you can off the **Zillow** listing prior to the call, including the aerial shot so you can see how the house is situated in the neighborhood (conrner lot, backing to busy street, etc.) Don't waste time and burn good will by asking for square footage and BR/BA counts. You can also check satellite images of the area on on **googleearth.com**, and zoom in from outer space. Ask about **condition**, what **upgrades** may have been put into the property, and you definitely want to get the **mortgage information** (we have a special way we ask for that in the scripts).

Also ask their **reason for moving**, many times that will give you a good indication of **how motivated they are**. If their reason for moving is a divorce or some other personal situation, we know that lends **urgency**. **How quickly** do they need to move is also a very key point, because if they need to move right away then you know there's more urgency. Check **the numbers** on the deal, payments, taxes, insurance, anything with a number attached needs to get verified as well.

Close the Deal. Here's the BIG ONE, why do you pick up the phone? What's the **purpose of the Closing Call? To Close the Deal!** This is where you work out the **4 "Pretty House" Deal Points**. We're talking about Creative Financing here, so there are things to be explained. They have to understand the financing will **remain in their name**. Don't drive out to a house if they don't understand that, or you'll be wasting a lot of time and gas. You must **cover the numbers and the main key points** of the deal, although don't think you have to hammer out every last detail. Some of that can and should happen in person at the house, just make sure they understand the deal at least in its broad strokes.

Negotiate the 4 Deal Points. Just follow our scripts to come to agreements here. Fortunately there is no better place to learn how to work out the price and terms than watching our calls on YouTube and in our systems. You also want to **answer any question or objection** that may come up.

You want to **walk them through the process** sometimes. This depends on their level of trust with you, and also their brain. If they're an engineer, a big "Thinker Brain, sometimes they really need you to take them through the process, **how this is going to work**. You can explain how they'll be going to the closing attorney (never "your attorney"), the paperwork that needs to be signed, and how the whole process will move forward.

The last one is give your **website address**. That's a credibility builder, and should help as a "Stick campaign".

Set the Appointment for the Deal Meeting. This is the second primary goal of every Closing Call. This is part of "**Asking for the Sale**". You want to be like a freight train at the beginning of this call, you want to be powering forward, chugga-chugga-chugga-chugga, all the way to get to the station (a set appointment). Do your best to get through the whole Closing Call Script all the way to Setting the Appointment. Appointments lead to Deal Meetings which lead to signed agreements & **big checks**!

That's where the money train begins, so **set the soonest possible time** for these appointments. If they'll see you in an hour and you can get out there in an hour with a typed agreement, get out there! **Time is of the essence** (as we always say).

Sign Off with Enthusiasm. You want to sign **on** and sign **off** with enthusiasm. People like to be around enthusiastic people, plus enthusiasm is contagious. Now we don't want you jumping over the moon about the house and saying, "Oh, this is exactly the house I want, it's *perfect*," until you have a deal in place with all the **terms decided upon**. What you can show plenty of enthusiasm about is the benefits of your deal to the seller.

You'll be tempted, but at the end **don't rehash the deal numbers**. You have it tentatively worked out, so don't poke that bear. At this point it's best to just type up the agreement with what you've got and get out there.

You may want to **set the seller's expectations** about any further negotiations (if that's necessary). Usually you're just heading out there to **buy their house now,** so they should know you intend to sign today.

Talk about **how great it's going to work out** for everybody, like we do. Our favorite word is *great*. "This is going to work out great. This will be great for you.

How great is this?" So what do you think they start thinking? They think it's going to be ***great!***

We also try to say **"Congratulations"** whenever it fits in. **Lynette loves this one!** Anytime you can have the sellers thinking, "This is a done deal," just from the Closing Call, that's great. Congratulations is great!

Being enthusiastic can carry you through any little rough patches or obstacles that are invariably going to come into your path. It'll help them "stay the course" as well, because they'll have caught your enthusiasm!

So those are all the **"Steps of the Closing Call"**. Learn this **most important part of the business** well, and you will be amply rewarded!

Preparation is in our **top Methods to Master Fear.** Here's the perfect form to get you mentally prepared to do effective closing calls. Either YOU or your Acquisitionist will fill out this form PRIOR to the Closing Call (contact us for a digital version). Only complete these for sellers who have shown flexibility on Terms ("Yes" leads).

CLOSING CALL PREP SHEET

Address:

_____

Seller: Phone:

_____

After Repaired Value: Repair Guesstimate:

_____

Maximum Allowable Offer: (MAO = ARV x 70% - Repairs)
(use for Cash Offers only)

_____

Mortgage Balance: Other Mortgages/Liens:

_____

Seller's "Hot Buttons" (needs/wants):

_____

Type of Deal, Exit Strategy:

_____

Financing Required:

_____

Deal #1 Price & Terms: use Assumptive Close, expect "Yes", use
Creative Financing Closing Call Script.

_____

Benefits to Seller: instant sale, debt relief, no commissions, no closing
costs, no showings no hassles, can move on, etc.

_____

Seller's Questions/Objections:

_____

Best Answers:

_____

Deal #2 / #3 Price & Terms: (back-up for Deal #1 if necessary)

_____

Notes:

_____

_____

_____

Creative Financing Deals/ "Terms" - Subject to, Sandwich Lease Purchase, Owner Financing, Option, Contract Assignment C.F. Exit Strategies - Lease-Purchase Buyer, Work-for-Equity, Owner Financed, Long-term L.P. Buyer, Cash-Out Buyer

CREATIVE FINANCING CLOSING CALL SCRIPT

(Start with the 4 Opening Questions)
1. *(have name)* Hi, I'm __ __, could I speak with ___ please?
1. *(no name)* Hi, I'm __ __, are you the person to talk with about the house for sale? ___ Great, and again my name is ___ ___, and what was your name? ____
2. I'm calling about the house, is it still for sale? ____ *(if spoke with VA or FSBO Caller)* I think you may have talked earlier with my assistant / partner ____.
3. Great, do you have a couple minutes to talk right now? *(Question #4 is first Rapport-Building Question, with goal to "**Make Friends**". It's easy & logical to ask about house, hoping that leads into "Friendlier" territory, unless you have a better opening on other topic – see Rapport-Building Scripts on 113.)*
4. So what can you tell me about the house? ___ OR
4. So what's the story on this house? ___ OR
4. *(Other, more friendly Rapport-Building question)*

Great, well we're definitely interested in buying your house. We buy and sell houses all around the area here, and when it's an ugly house, we usually pay all cash. Now with a nicer (higher quality) house like yours, the way we would usually buy it is through Owner Financing or with a Lease Purchase. That just means you give us a little bit of time to pay you off in full. Do you think something like that might work out for you, *(first name)*?

How long do you need? *(do not say this unless asked)*
The longer the better, but usually at least a couple years. Of course that means we can pay top price, so do you think that might work for you, _____?

A. *(Seller says "Yes")* Okay, that's great. **OR**

B. (If soft "Yes" or "Maybe") The great thing is, when you're open to giving us a little time, we can usually pay top price for the house, even full price. So what kind of shape is the house in? _____

Working Out the 4 Deal Points (we have much more detailed & case-specific **Closing Call Scripts**, perfect for working out the 4 Deal Points, in our Wolff-LeGrand **"What to Say & Do"** System. Call Us at 888-Rich-Now!)

PURCHASE PRICE – So in terms of your asking price, if we work this out and close whenever you want, what's the least you'll take? _____ Is that the best you can do? ___

MONTHLY PAYMENT – I see your payment is __, so we can cover that every month. (No payment, see other Scripts)

TERM – Some sellers are okay with giving us 30 years, they like the monthly payment. Others can only do shorter terms like 5 years. What's the longest that could work for you?

DOWN PAYMENT – Now the way we usually work it is that you'll get your first check from us when we start making monthly payments to you after we close. You understand that, right?

(All Negotiation of 4 Deal Points here, can settle for "ranges")

Great. Well it sounds like you're open, you're flexible on giving us a little time to pay you off in full, so I'd like to go ahead and set up an appointment to see the house. We can't buy the house without seeing it, right? (smile)

So we'll just come out and meet with you, and we'll bring along a Standard Agreement, and if everything looks good are you ready to move forward right now? _____ Very good! When would work best for you? _____ (Time is of an essence, make it ASAP)

I'm really looking forward to meeting with you then. Take care!

50 CLOSING CALLS CHECKLIST

Start Date _____ Goal Completion Date _____
Actual Completion Date _____
Reward(s) _____
Write in date/time of each call. Type of deal, other notes optional.

1.				
				10!
				20!
				30!
				40!
				50!!!

There are **many Action Steps** that go into building and running a successful Real Estate Investing business. You can be mediocre at all of them, and still make great money if you are really good at <u>one</u>. That one Action Step is making **Closing Calls!** When you can get "**A**'s" on your Closing Calls you will make a lot of money!

Do you want to **choose where you end up in life?** If your answer is "Yes", then you must choose wisely how you spend your minutes today. **You are creating your future right now.** Right now, and every right now after that until the end. When you choose to **spend 1 to 2 hours each week making Closing Calls**, you're devoting your time to the single **most productive and financially rewarding Action Step** that is available to you in life.

3. Deal Meeting

We've repeatedly said the most important 15 minutes of every deal you do is the Closing Call. Maybe we haven't sufficiently stressed **the vital nature of the Deal Meeting!** This is the **20-60 minutes** that can actually **make the deal all come together, or all fall apart.**

When do you need to be at your **most prepared**? When do you need to **execute at the highest level**? When can a few words **make or break** the Deal? What is a real **"Moment of Truth"** in every Deal? <u>**ANSWER**</u>: The <u>Deal Meeting</u>!

The Deal Meeting can actually be kind of scary! You're not sure what to expect, there are always unknowns, and your hopes are sky high. The first few sidewalks you head up with an agreement in hand, undoubtedly your heart will just about be beating out of your chest!

We created **"20 Instant Methods to Master Fear"** (we do a whole presentation on it at our **"Changing Your Life Workshop"**, which you and a guest can come to for FREE by calling 888-Rich-Now, we do 3 per year)!)

One of the most powerful Methods is **"Preparation!"** When facing Fear, count on your *Training and Preparation!* Brian was a loyal Boy Scout, and the Boy Scout Motto is **"Be Prepared."** If you blow a deal on a Closing Call or in a Deal Meeting, it's almost always because you went in unprepared.

Vital to Proper Preparation is your understanding of these **30 Steps of the Deal Meeting**, as well as our crucial **"Deal Meeting Script"** that follows. Also you want to review your (hopefully extensive) **NOTES** from your Closing Call. Remember our favorite Chinese proverb, **"The faintest ink is better than the best memory."**

Always take **4 Types of NOTES**;

1. About House
2. About Deal
3. About Prospect, Personal Notes (vital)
4. Verbatim Notes inside "quotation marks", exact words, usually about numbers or very important Deal Notes.

The 30 Steps of the Deal Meeting can be broken into 2 Parts – **15 Prep Steps**, and the actual **15 Steps of the Deal Meeting**. Knowing these steps will boost your Conversion Ratio & revolutionize your Investing Career!

15 PREP STEPS FOR THE DEAL MEETING

1. **Clean Vehicle** – This is vital for Professionalism. It doesn't need to be a Mercedes, but it must be neat and clean. Otherwise it can adversely affect your credibility.

2. **Attractive Outfit** -- Dress like the better Realtors in your area. Maybe even buy a new outfit, you'll feel more confident, and perform like your Best Self!

3. **Well-Groomed** – Comb or brush hair, trim beard or shave, re-apply make-up (especially lipstick), smell nice.

4. **Professional Business Cards** – These give you great **confidence and credibility**, they should look like a nice Realtor card. You're more memorable when you put a professional picture of yourself on the front. Walk into Deal Meetings like a professional, with card in hand. On your card it says that you buy and sell houses, the name of LLC/company, your website, and your phone number. If you don't have this professional card to hand out you are at a disadvantage. Pay for upgraded card stock, plus full color. Use correct messaging on the back from the sample on page 88, and also found in our Wolff-LeGrand **"Masterful Marketing System"**.

5. **Legal-Sized Portfolio** – executive-style, maybe gold corners, don't fold legal-sized agreements

6. **Typed Agreements** – Take the time to present your offer truly professionally, which means typed. After the Closing Call you want to type in **4 Pretty House Deal Points**

   1) Purchase Price
   2) Monthly Payment
   3) Length of Term
   4) Down Payment

   If necessary you will sometimes give Seller a small down payment. It gives them another reason to do it.

7. **Blank Agreements** – These are not addressed, you want a completely blank Standard Purchase & Sales Agreement, and a blank Lease with Option Agreement. These are your back-ups, you should start over fresh if you end up having to change 3 or more of the 4 Deal Points at the Deal Meeting (it happens).

8. **Buying Packets** – Whole collection of paperwork for Buying (i.e.; Authorization to Release Information, etc.) When you have **5** Buying Packets ready you are Prepared!

9. **Review Zillow/RealEstateABC.com/County Recorder** – Get all the info on the house, especially on Zillow under the **Price/Tax History Tab** *(when last Sold, for how much, to who, etc.—only in Disclosure states)*, plus top 2 accurate "Comps" from RealEstateABC.com.

10. **Review Any Notes** – from yourself on Closing Call or VA/FSBO Caller's Notes from the Opening Call.

11. **Use Mapquest** (or Other App) -- Plan Route and Timing to Deal Meeting.

12. **Read through the "Deal Meeting Script"** – **Aloud** and/or **Role-Play** if Possible

13. **Leave Early** -- to Arrive Early & More Stress-FREE

14. **Do Our "Psych Up"** in the Car *(not right in front of house)* – pump fists while chanting **"I Am A Successful Real Estate Investor, YES YES YES!"**

15. **Approach Door** with Confidence!!!

15 STEPS OF THE DEAL MEETING

1) **Greet with Enthusiasm** – Be ready when the door opens with a big smile and warm handshake. **First Impressions make or break Deals.** Be as Upbeat as you can, remember that this is an exercise in human psychology and you want to generate positive feelings! Be quick to hand them your Professional Business Card.

2) **Build In-Person Rapport** – Whatever Rapport you've built on the Closing Call, now's the time to **bring it home** and **monetize that love!** You should have plenty of Notes to work with, since you've been applying that **new Habit** of always **taking 60+ seconds of Notes** immediately after hanging up from the Closing Call. Try to use a Personal Note from your Closing Call Prep Sheet, spouse/child/pet names always **go over big!** Introduce yourself and include them immediately if you've not spoken with them before.

3) **House Tour** – Walk through the property, convey Professionalism by taking good notes in your Portfolio (you'll appreciate them later). You may also take video or pictures. **Compliments** are very important, mostly stick to design choices and family pictures.

4) **Sit Down at a Table** – A good line to remember is, "Why don't we start at the kitchen and end at the kitchen?" Either there or the dining room, **pick the best table.** Try not to sit in anybody's "usual spot", ask first. Otherwise they could be uncomfortable the whole meeting, and you're trying to **raise their comfort level.** Whatever you do, don't plant yourselves in the living room across an expanse of carpet from each other. You **need to be near**, where you can guide them through the agreement close-up.

Remember you are **in the Endgame** now, not just of the Deal Meeting but of the whole Buying Process. **Getting the Agreement in front of the Seller with a pen in their hand**, that is your **Endgame Goal!**

When you have not yet totally solidified all 4 Pretty House Deal Points, then this is when and where you do it. Then you **"Ask for the Sale"**, and at the Deal Meeting that means pointing to the bottom line and saying something like, "Okay, now you just put your autograph right there." **Walk out with a signed agreement** and you have met your Goal!

5) **Question and Answer Period** *(optional)*. If you've already answered a lot of questions then you don't have to ask for more. If only one spouse was there for some of the meeting you may need to open it up. Refer to the combination of your Closing Call Scripts with Objection Answers and our Deal Meeting Script here.

6) **Review the Agreement** with the Seller(s). Don't get too bogged down, move briefly through the clauses, you don't need to cover every item.

7) **Typical "Asks" from Seller** – Always ask for Appliances, ask for any other large furniture or other items they might just as soon leave behind. Also ask if they could do any specified **minor repairs** before you take possession (if it won't affect the Deal).

8) **Q & A II**, the Sequel – "Now that we've gone through the Agreement, do you have any other questions?"

9) **Give the Seller "Consideration"** – Turn over $10 or $100 ($100 feels more Professional). This is the amount written under 1A in the agreement, and they MUST sign at the bottom of the contract as evidence they received the Consideration.

10) ***<u>Show Seller Where to Sign</u>!*** -- Get a pen in their hand and the Agreement in front of them. Don't chicken out, this is the **Endgame**, the **"Moment of Truth"**!

11) **Complete the Other Paperwork** – Fill out and get signed the remainder of the applicable documents. You will be sending the signed Agreement ASAP to your attorney or title agent,

whoever generates title reports for you. Have the Seller sign a "Lender Letter" if there is an underlying mortgage on the property. Get a testimonial!

12) **Help the Seller Release the Zillow Listing** – There are 2 Steps to this, they have to mark it Sold and also release it. Remember you will be turning this property around as soon as you get clean title back, so you don't want your big **"1-Hour Open House"** to be spoiled by an old and incorrect Zillow Listing. **Zillow is powerful**, a necessary and a GREAT way to market all your properties.

13) **Collect Seller's Documents** -- Mortgage Paperwork, Insurance, Homeowners Association, etc. Take pictures or leave them copies. Ensure there's **no balloon payment or adjustable rate mortgage** that will disrupt profitability. Use the Checklist in our D.U.F.U.S. System or on the Gold Club to know exactly what to collect.

14) **Explain the Next Steps** – Let them know your expectations of them, where they have to be, what they have to do, and what happens next – Title Report, any possible inspection, upcoming Appointment with the Closing Attorney, etc.

15) **Depart with Enthusiasm** – **"Congratulations,** you just sold your house, you can get on with your life, **ISN'T THIS GREAT**?!! It's been such a pleasure meeting with you both in person, this is going to work out great for you guys!"

So that's it! Follow these simple Steps, plus the script here, and soon you'll be getting Sellers' signatures on bottom lines at your very own Deal Meetings!

DEAL MEETING SCRIPT

When you park in front of the house be aware the Sellers can see you, and may be evaluating your professionalism and your vehicle. Approach the door with positive energy, ring doorbell or knock. When they answer smile big, gracefully reach to shake their hand.

When you park in front of the house be aware the Sellers can see you, and may be evaluating your professionalism and your vehicle. Approach the door with positive energy, ring doorbell or knock. When they answer smile big, gracefully reach to shake their hand.

Hi, it's _____ _____, you must be _____. So great to meet you (both) in person. We had such a good talk on the phone, it's nice to put a face to your voice. (Stepping in) So how are you today?__ I'm doing great, thank you. Here's my card. (hand them cards)

Build face-to-face Rapport by bringing up a personal reference using the notes from your Closing Call Prep Sheet. Effective references include pets, shared interests, or **compliments** on the home lay-out, their design choices, family pictures, or personal appearance/outfit (careful). Pet the pet if possible.

Your house is very nice, I really like _____. Can we just take a look around, do a little tour of the house? We could start in the kitchen, and then we'll end in the kitchen, how's that? (kitchen or dining room, pick the best table). Great.

Take video or pictures, also **take notes** on a pad or an I-pad (lists include features to mention in ads, repairs, items to ask for beyond appliances). If the Seller already has very good pictures on Zillow or Craigslist sometimes you can use those. Continue complimenting features of the house, small design touches, family pictures, etc...

Okay great, well I've had a good look at the house. Why don't we just sit here at the table together and look over a few numbers? Do you have any regular spot(s) where you like to sit? Great, I'll just sit here then. Do you think I could get a little water, please? Thanks so much. So when we talked on the phone, we figured out several things. That's what I went by to fill out this Standard Purchase Agreement /Lease Purchase Agreement. *(hold up Agreement)* You can see it's pretty simple, just one page.

Starting right here at the top, this is us as the buyer, and you're listed here as the seller. Do I have your name(s) spelled right? Now there's no one else on the title to the house, is that correct? Good. And of course here's the property location right here.

Now we'll go through the rest of the agreement together, most of it is just standard stuff, and I'll point out the important parts. Now here we get into the numbers…

Proceed through the agreement, and the terms that you'd agreed upon. At the end say something like, "And this is where you sign right here." (Asking for the Sale)

For more detailed scripting, plus in-depth deal structuring and analysis, see our truly incredible **"Pretty House Power Pack"** *referenced here. You really need to take the next step with us and* **order** *that system, the information's on the next page. Stick with us, we want to help you* **Change Your Life!**

You're reading the book, now it's
Time to Take Action!

Call Our Office Now or
Go to the Website Below to Order Our Amazing

"Pretty House Power Pack"
(Retail Price $497) ONLY $97!
with CODE below)

Entire Manual on Pretty House Deals
Online Videos/Audios OR DVD & CD
- All the Tools You Need

Start Closing Creative Financing Deals TODAY!
Make Huge Option Deposits FAST, Earn Passive Monthly Cash
Flow, Build Long-Term Wealth!

CALL 888-Rich-Now
(1-888-742-4669)
OR go to *PrettyHousePower.com*
Save $400 w/ **Coupon Code FSF400PHPP**

Limited Number of Systems Available
ACT NOW So You Don't Miss Out!

Alton & Rocio Jones - *Long Beach, CA*

An acquaintance explained to me that she was "Sick And Tired" of her property management guy ripping her off, and that she had not received rent on her units in over 6 months.

OPPORTUNITY! The seller has 5 SFR All 3 bed and 2 bath homes that are all Free and Clear. I asked what was she looking to get for the properties. Eventually we got a $25,000 price reduction, because I asked.

When everyone else was having fun on the 4th of July, I was out closing 5 deals for my family.

The numbers: Zero Down and Zero interest and No Payment for 90 days. $100,000 equity today, $1200.00 Cash Flow over 5 years = $79,920 In 5 1/2 years. Free & Clear and over $200,00.00 in equity.

Thanks to Lynette and Brian Wolff, who taught us how to do this and have helped our business greatly!

Also just received another check for $55,000 on another deal. We had none of our money and only our name on the contract for 90 days. This is the biggest "Shut Up heck" we have ever received. We are looking forward to making many more checks like this!

Chapter 6
The System Is the Solution
Automation and Delegation

Automation just means that things run ***automatically***.

The two components required for this are effective **Organizational Systems** like the one below, and **Delegation**. One of our nicknames is **"The King and Queen of Automation & Delegation"**, so we love training investors on these subjects.

We actually created an entire program on this, check it out at *The-WolffCouple.com*. It features great training, checklists, flow charts, and more! Thinker Brains love it! We'll start with this simple but precise Organizational System for your office paper flow, then follow up with more on Delegation.

Steps of Deal File Organization

Here's a clear explanation of the system and some of the forms to use to organize your office and your deals in progress. It's best to keep it as simple as possible so you don't get tangled up in paperwork, or start over-thinking and wasting time on this part of the business.

Step 1: Get **3** standing file racks. Rack #1 holds File Folders #1, #2, and #3. Rack #2 holds Property Files in progress. Rack #3 holds Buyer Leads.

Step 2: Label one File Folder "#1—Intake Sellers", and another one "#2—Intake Buyers". All lead sheets—Seller Info Scripts, FSBO Call Scripts, Property Information forms, answering service forms, Pretty or Ugly House Buyer Info Scripts, all Lead sheets go into one of these 2 file folders.

Step 3: Go through these folders daily, and pre-screen out the obvious Suspects. Put them into #3 File Folder labeled "Suspects". Pick a time on the same day each week to scan through and see if any are worth calling. Spend almost no time on the phone here, be quick to say "Thanks anyway, bye."

Step 4: Schedule a time each night to call the Prospects in File #1 and File #2. Pre-screen to figure out what type of Seller or Buyer you are dealing with by using our Pre-Screening Guide. Use the matching Closing Call Scripts in the "What to Say" Manuals.

Step 5: The lead sheets that don't result in an appointment go into either File Folder #3, Suspects, or your Follow-Up File Box/Drawer. Your Follow-Up Box/Drawer is set up with 31 file folders, labeled 1-31, signifying dates of the month. Depending on your Closing Call conversation, put them in the appropriate file (i.e. If today is the 1st and you want to call them back in a week, put them in file folder 8.) Check Follow-Ups from this special file each day.

Step 6: For leads resulting in appointments or calls for further action, give them their own file. Label the file with the Property Address (i.e. 1234 Jones St.) Attach the matching Step by Step Checklist to the in-side front cover, and keep track of what stage the deal is by writing in dates for each completed Action Step. *Make sure to type same info into Deal Organization Chart.*

Print off a "Comment Log" from our "20 Must-Have Forms" data CD, and put it in the file. Put all paperwork (lead sheet, comps, title report, contracts, interested Buyer file, flyers, etc) into this file folder. Put property files in File Rack #2, and waiting qualified Buyers in File Rack #3. Once a Buyer shows interest in one place, move their file into the property file.

<u>Step 7</u>: When a deal is closed and the Buyer has taken residence, move file into a Closed Deals File Box/Drawer. Have a separate section for Lease-Purchase and Work for Equity Buyers, because they will require ongoing servicing. As needed, buy more file racks, boxes, and drawers *That's a **good** thing!*

Now that we've covered the basics of **Organization**, let's turn to **Delegation!** This **list** covers the **Key Team Members** to whom you'll be **Delegating**, plus the **Duties** you'll be delegating to them, and the most important **Prescreening Questions** to ask. Often you can get good referrals from other investors at your local Real Estate Investing Association (**REIA**) Meetings. We recommend you attend *(plus you'll look smart if you carry this book)!*

MY DREAM TEAM

Printer
Main Duty – Print marketing materials
What do you charge for different kinds of business cards? How long would it take to get them?
What do you charge for black ink on colored 8 ½" x 11" paper? (4 cent flyers are good)

Title Agent
Main Duty – Pull title reports, Closings?
How quickly can you pull a title report? (2-3 days is good in most areas)
Since I'll be sending you all my business, would you be able to order reports for me for free/at a good discount?

Insurance Agent
Main Duty– Insure properties against loss
What are your rates for landlord insurance?
Do you have any issues with keeping the original mortgagee as a loss payee on the policy? (underlying mtg)

Can you write insurance policies on vacant houses? (i.e. during a re-hab)

Real Estate Attorney
Duties – Evictions, Closings
Have you worked much with investors?
Are you comfortable with owner financing deals, or lease purchase deals? How about land trusts?
What do you charge to send out notices? (to pay or vacate, eviction, etc.)
How quickly can you usually schedule Closing Appts?

Mortgage Broker
Main Duties– Pull credit, get mortgages
How many different lenders do you work with?
What's the lowest credit score and highest debt ratio that you can get approved for a mortgage right now?
Do you have any special programs working well now?

Realtors
Main Duties – Find deals on MLS, run Comps
Do you work with many investors?
Do you deal mainly with pretty houses or ugly houses? You worked w/ Lease Purchases or Owner Financing? Can you find good deals on ugly houses now in MLS? Can you do search for all properties in my "farm area" listed at $20+ below average price per sq ft in the area?
Can you do an MLS search for me for all properties that have just gone over 120/90/60 days listed? Also expired properties?
(Warm up Realtor before getting to advanced requests. Eventually you'll want these lists often for marketing).

Hard Money Lenders
Duty– Money for Rehabs/Short Sales
How quickly can you close? (certainly within 30 days, best if under 10 days)

What is the highest L.T.V.* that you go? (*Loan To Value Percentage -- 70% is usually best, 65% common)

Private Money Lenders

Duty – Money to buy & fix

Have you ever invested in real estate?

Do you have capital that you could put out right now for a high return, and guaranteed by real estate?

Contractors As Needed for

Main Duties – Property Upgrades, Upkeep, Miscellaneous

- a. General Cleaning
- b. Painting
- c. Carpet Cleaning
- d. Flooring (carpet, laminate, upgraded flooring)
- e. Window Coverings
- f. General Home Repairs
- g. Plumbing
- h. Roofing
- i. Landscaping
- j. Yard Maintenance (mowing)
- k. Snow Removal
- l. Junk Removal
- m. Pest Inspection
- n. Pest Control
- o. Pool Maintenance
- p. Home Inspection
- q. Locksmith
- r. Residential Alarm
- s. Credit Repair
- t. R.E. Auctioneer

ACQUISITIONIST MAIN JOB DUTIES

1. Generate/Collect Incoming Lead Sheets   2 hrs/wk
   Make Outbound Calls take/respond to
   incoming calls   1 hr

2. Make Closing Calls, Set Appointments.   3-10 hrs+/wk

3. Keep Detailed Notes on   2 hrs
   Closing Call Prep Sheets.

4. Research properties, compute Comps   2 hrs

5. Complete Agreements and Documents.   3 hrs

6. Do Deal Meetings, Get Documents Signed.   8 hrs
   2+/week, with commutes

7. Use D.U.F.U.S. to Follow Up on All Leads.   2 hrs

8. Maintain Adequate Organization.   1 hr

Blair H. - *Clemmons, NC*

I just completed my first "pretty house deal" and brought home my first five- figure check! To say this event has changed my life is an understatement. For the past seven months I've grown personally, financially, and spiritually through this process of getting to this point.

When I started I was physically shaking with fear, but I knew that if I didn't get over this hump, my life would never change and I'd be stuck in my dead-end career forever.

I received a call and went to the house of a seller named Tammy. It was clear she was not going to let me leave without me buying her house - a very well-kept 3BR/2BA with a deck on the back, a nice yard, nice area. It was perfect.

She was going on disability, she was scared, and had been praying for a solution. I almost cried when she told me I was the answer to her prayers. We got the paperwork done and when I left her house this whole business suddenly just CLICKED for me. There's no other way to describe it.

All of a sudden I had 100% clarity on everything the Wolffs had been teaching me and telling me all these months. It was a major turning point in my life that I'll never forget. You know how you hear Brian on stage talking about all this stuff, and it almost seems too good to be true? But I'm here to tell you that it's ALL TRUE. Every word of it. I bought the house subject to a $91k first mortgage with a $730/mo payment, plus $1500 cash to the seller to help her move into her new apartment.

Less than a week after closing I got a buyer who loved the house and put $20,000 down. She is ecstatic that she was able to buy this house even though no bank would give her a loan.

She now has a beautiful new home for her and her daughter, and her life has changed dramatically because of it.

This past Friday I left the attorney's office with a $20,000 check in my hand and a completely new outlook on life, on business, on myself, and on my future.

After the turning point I had when it all clicked for me, I went from one deal every 2-3 months to now picking up four contracts in the past four weeks, and a fifth one I'm picking up tomorrow. I've now hired an assistant to help me keep up with all of this, and I'm delegating more and more to her every day.

I sleep very well knowing my future is looking 10 times brighter than before, my assistant loves her new career, I'm helping home sellers with some of the worst situations in their lives, and helping buyers get into homes they otherwise wouldn't be able to buy.

Brian and Lynette, you have changed my life and my family's life forever, and I can't thank you enough. I thank God that He brought us together and He gave me the courage and persistence to stick with it and follow-through. This is a whole new world, and I'm so very grateful!

Dixie & Brandon Roza - *Springfield, MO*

Thanks to the Wolffs' motivational program, we kept pushing forward into this new world of pretty houses, coming from the flipping, work-really-hard world. The Wolffs teach you what to say, how to say it, so much great information!

Thank you for getting us to focus on building the whole company while our automation is working for us! Prior to this program we would meet every buyer and every seller and make multiple phone calls to talk to everyone and get nothing else done! Now we're making big, regular checks and we've done dozens of deals! We're making hundreds of thousands of dollars per year in real estate now. Thank you so much for changing our lives!

Chapter 7
Sell Now with the "1-Hour Sale"!

There are huge paydays in Real Estate Investing. It's **made more Millionaires** than any other business in history. So as an investor, when do you start getting those huge checks? When do you see the **massive profits** that will make you a Millionaire?

WHEN YOU SELL!

Your **Buyers** write you your **huge paychecks**. That's what's so exciting about the selling side of investing, it's when you **<u>Get Paid</u>**! Imagine someone just handing you a check for **$20,000**! And if that's possible, then why not have 2 or 3 people every month handing you checks like that? Let's look at how you can set up a **Machine** that churns out those huge checks for you every month!

We *LOVE* **the selling side** of the Pretty House business, where you **collect big checks** from **Lease Purchase Buyers**. After over a decade and a half of teaching real estate investing, what have we found to be the chief reasons people don't succeed?

2 Main Pretty House Career Killers

1. Fear of Talking to Sellers
2. Fear of *"Pulling the Trigger"* and Buying

We addressed the first challenge in Chapter 5 on "What You Say", now here's where we conquer the second. When you have a true system in place to sell fast, a **Home Selling Machine**, it fills you with confidence.

The fear disappears when you have **qualified buyers** with **huge checks** waiting for you to find them new homes!

You'll be **massively motivated** to get on the phone with sellers, and you'll be pulling every trigger you can! Armed with the knowledge that **a big check is just waiting** for you, nothing will hold you back!

We want to give you supreme confidence by teaching you exactly how to build your own "Million Dollar Machine". Whether you like looking at numbers or not, you're going to **love these numbers**:

The Million Dollar Machine
Goal -- **3** Pretty House Deals per Month

Cash Now = $30,000 - $90,000+ Can Spend Immediately
> **3** *Non-Refundable Option Deposits, $10,000 - $30,000*
Cash Later = $60,000 - $150,000+ in Home Equity
> **3** *Back End Paydays, $20,000 - $50,000 each*
Cash Flow = $300 - $1500+ in Passive Income
> **3** *Monthly Rent Payments, with NO Repairs*

Average Profit per Deal = **$30,000** *(example below shows Average $10,000 down, $20,000 back end)*
3 Deals per Month X **12** Months = **36** Deals per Year

36 Deals X $10,000 Average Option Deposit =
$360,000 Instant CASH!
36 Deals X $20,000 Average Back End Profit =
$720,000 Growing Wealth
36 Deals X $300 Average Monthly Cash Flow =
$10,800 Passive Income/Month

Total Profit in CASH and EQUITY =
$1,080,000 in ONE YEAR + Cash Flow

The Million Dollar Machine produces multiple deals monthly, big cash in a little time, and *your dream life!*

We hope you really grasp the gravity of these numbers, and the fact that they could be **real for you**. Even with a much more modest goal of 1 deal per month, you're still looking at over **$350,000** profit per year!

But to keep the Million Dollar Machine running, what is crucial? What is the biggest threat, what is the main **BOTTLENECK** that can clog up the Machine?

*Holding Homes That **Won't Sell!** --* 30, 60, 90+ Days

Some beginning investors are so scared of this that **they can't pull the trigger** on their first deal. They have what we call *"First Deal-itis"*. We understand, because about 15 years ago we went through the same exact fears.

6 FEARS Over Not Selling Fast

1. Making Payments on a Vacant House
2. Stuck Long-Term with a "Money Pit"
3. Wasted Hours & Weekends Trying to Sell
4. Disappointing the Seller, Losing the Deal
5. One House Sucks Up All Time for Investing
6. Living Under Constant Stress

What is the truly **Scary Result?** Your marketing to buy houses stops, and your whole **business grinds to a halt!** You aren't closing multiple deals per month, you're lucky to close one deal every few months.

You only need to find **3** Lease Purchase Buyers per month with $10,000 or more down to have your own **Million Dollar Machine**. So what's *the secret* to finding and closing these Buyers? The simple truth is, **Buyers buy on emotion**. Desire is certainly part of it, but we have a special name for the most intense emotion they feel. We call it **"F.O.M.O." -- Fear Of Missing Out**.

To sell fast you need to *"foment the F.O.M.O."* by building a sense of **URGENCY** in your Buyers. The absolute best way to do that is… The **1-Hour Open House** Plan!

Your goal is to drive a **thunderous herd** of prospects to the Open House, where they bid on the highest down payment! Do it **our way** to always **sell fast**, and also find **multiple buyers** from each Open House. Plus you'll even have **fun** and **excitement** while you make **huge paydays!**

Benefits from 1-Hour Open Houses

- ☐ Takes Care of **Steps #4-7** of the "10 Steps to Sell Homes" in minutes instead of hours
- ☐ Builds a 6-Figure **Buyers List** in 1 Weekend
- ☐ Gives You the Confidence to Offer and Pay Pretty House Sellers **Full Price**
- ☐ Pulls In the **Most** Possible **CASH Down** on Lease Purchase Deals
- ☐ Floods Your Business with **Qualified Buyers**
- ☐ Grows a Massive **Referral Base** for FREE Deals
- ☐ Helps **Eliminate Vacancies** AND **Repairs!**
- ☐ Builds $10,000 per Month **Passive Income** in 1 Year
- ☐ Gives Peace of Mind When Many of Your Homes Are **Sold Before You Buy** Them

When you start using the *1-Hour Open House* Strategy it will change your whole approach to investing, and **wipe away the fear**. Knowing you can reliably sell your Pretty Houses for huge profits (in 1 hour) gives you **the confidence you need** as an investor. This exciting Exit Strategy/Marketing Strategy is the primary way to sell houses fast in today's market. This System will empower YOU to build **your own Million Dollar Machine!**

Alecia Phillips - *Minneapolis, MN*

I wanted to send you a quick letter thanking you for your "1-Hour Sale" System. We implemented our first open house using the system, we advertised just like you suggested, and held the open house on a Saturday for 1 hour only. At the start of the open house we had about

30 people waiting on the doors to open! Thank goodness I had help to run the open house with me, because I wouldn't have been able to handle that amount of traffic by myself. The result — we had a ton of interest from the open house, and we selected a tenant/buyer who put $20,000 down!

The 1-Hour Sale System is going to make selling our properties so much easier, and allow us to cherry-pick the buyers with the highest option deposits. We love the feeding frenzy that the open house creates when we follow the system.

It really forces the legitimate buyers to either commit to buying or risk missing out on the house.

We've attached a picture of the exterior, and a copy of the check from closing (we collected 3k down and the $17,000 balance at closing with our real estate attorney). Thanks again for the awesome system!

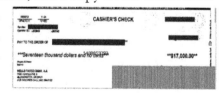

10 STEPS TO SELLING A HOME

1. Get "Pretty House" **Ready to Sell**
   --Clean up and/or complete repairs, Stage home
   --Special Staging for "1-Hour Sale" Open House

2. Set Up Your Buyer **Incoming Call Capture**
   --Answering Service, Assistant, You, Voicemail

3. **Market for Buyers** Using 4+ Different Methods
   --signs, internet, door hangers, Facebook, etc.
   --Market Open House thru "1-Hour Sale" System
   For Open Houses, follow "Open House Guide"

4. Take and Make **Opening Calls**
   --Use "Pretty House Buyer Opening Call Script"
   build rapport, establish credibility, gather info

5. **Prescreen Buyers**
   Sort by 2 Main Factors, Quality and Category
   Follow Prescreening Guide ("What to Do" Manual)
   and the "Responses to Buyers Guide"

6. Make **Closing Calls** to prospects, set appointments

7. Do **Deal Meetings**
   Get paperwork signed, collect docs and check

8. Schedule Signing Appointment, get Total **Deposit**

9. Wrap up the **Details** of the Transaction.

10. Turn over **Possession** of Home to Tenant Buyer

*Steps 4 – 7 (Opening Call, Prescreening, Closing Call, Deal Meeting)
can all be conducted at Open Houses.

PROPERTY MARKETING PLAN for _____

Marketing Method	Units	Cost (approx.)
Signs – Lease Purchase Program	_____	_____
Signs – Directional "Pointer"	_____	_____
Zillow Listing *w/ Open House*	____1____	FREE
Craigslist Ads	_____	FREE
Facebook Ads	_____	_____
Facebook Groups	Ongoing	FREE
Newspapers w/ Internet Sites	_____	_____
Door Hangers / Flyers	_____	_____
Business Cards	Ongoing	_____
Referrals	Ongoing	_____
Other	_____	_____
Total	_____	_____

Notes:

_____

_____

_____

_____

OPEN HOUSES

Your Primary Home Marketing Method
Lynette & Brian talk Open Houses & Urgency

Why are Open Houses such an important part of the Selling Plan?

It all comes down to building a sense of Urgency.

Now we will tell you that most "traditional" Open Houses don't work. Some Realtor sitting out there in some big lonely empty house -- there's no sense of urgency, is there? Maybe one or two people wander in sporadically, but the way we structure and market our Open Houses we build a massive amount of urgency. So when they DO work, WHY do they work? Because...

BUYERS BUY ON EMOTION!

A sense of Urgency really riles up the Buyers' emotions. Sellers aren't like this because they can't just decide to hand you their house, there's a process. But with Buyers, can you get them all worked up and have them make a decision and just hand you a check?

Absolutely.

So when we say Buyers make decisions on emotion, what emotion is it? There is always some Desire for the house, but mostly it's usually Fear. FOMO we call it -- the Fear Of Missing Out.

Let's say you're a Buyer, and you've looked at 50 houses and you've already missed out on the last 3 because you acted too slow, plus your bad credit sure doesn't help. Yet still, here is this beautiful home and you can have it right now and even get help to own it...if you hand over a big deposit check before that guy over in the corner there talking to his wife does.

HUGE SENSE OF URGENCY.

Huge F.O.M.O., <u>F</u>ear <u>O</u>f <u>M</u>issing <u>O</u>ut.

That's how Open Houses build that urgency. The more people you can get in there over that 1 hour the more urgency and FOMO.

We want you to get lots of Buyers processed through your system, and you want to crank up the excitement and spectacle and overall "busy-ness". That's the whole key. The reason that we put up big splashy signs and flags and streamers is that it helps builds that Urgency.

So that's what our Open Houses look like.

We have a whole elaborate display package available, with a diagram and instructions to set it up. I actually did a lot of work to find this awesome sign company, it's been in Phoenix for over 50 years, and they do nothing but realty signs. They helped me put together the package with these huge 15 foot "swooper" flags, gold foil streamers, and lots of signs.

Do you think that generates some urgency and some excitement? Absolutely.

We bargained a great discount for you guys on that if you're interested, there is a certificate with a special code in our "1-Hour Sale" System to order that display package.

So how many people do you want to show up at your Open Houses?

I would say if you can get 20 people in there, 20 or more people at the same time, and there's 2 or 3 qualified ones in there, then that's the success formula you're looking for.

Ideally it's even more people, closer to 50.

You want as many people as possible, even "Lookie Lou's". With all that action and people milling around, the Buyers are all worked up with Urgency.

They want the house, and there you are saying all the best words from the Open House Closer Script.

And just like magic, there you are in less than an hour holding a big check from a qualified Buyer.

When Lynette was a new home sales agent they had a nickname for her, the *"Urgency Expert"*.

You always want to keep that internal sense of Urgency in mind when *you're* talking to Buyers, especially at Open Houses.

It's vital to be able to instill a sense of Urgency in Buyers -- through your signage, your Open House display kit, your prize drawing, the crowd you attract, and the scripts you and your Closer and Greeter use.

That is a huge key to success!

Creating Ugency is one powerful benefit of our "1-Hour Open Houses", and another is that Open Houses very efficiently check off Steps 4 through 7 on the "10 Steps to Selling a Home". The Open House takes care of the Opening Call, Prescreening, the Closing Call, and the Deal Meeting!

All 4 steps, done incorrectly that can sometimes take weeks, all 4 knocked out in 5-10 minutes.

That's the way to build *scalability*, when you can so efficiently line up Buyers not just for one home, but for more homes to come.

That's how you close multiple deals per month and make millions!

10 STEPS FOR CLOSER AT OPEN HOUSE

1. Make sure home is **Staged & Ready** for Open House.

2. Coordinate with Open House **Greeter** (when present).

3. Greet and **Build Rapport** with incoming Visitors.

4. Have all Visitors fill out a **Registration Card**, OR "**Next Step**" Form (all Forms in "1-Hour Sale" System).

5. **Identify Quality Prospects** using written answers and **5 Pre-screening Questions.**
   - Quality Prospect = 5%+ down payment, can afford monthly payment
   - Prescreen out Tenant Buyers with less than 2% of purchase price for down payment.

6. Enthusiastically show attractive Home Features to Quality Prospects on **guided Home Tours**.

7. Go through **Closing Meeting Script** with good Buyers.

8. Answer **Questions and Objections** from the Buyer until they are ready to Close.

9. **Complete 4 Documents** to Sell on Lease Purchase.

10. Collect initial **Non-Refundable Option Deposit(s)** from Prospects. Get $5000+, the rest by Attorney. You have permission to take back-up down payments, just find extra Buyers homes too!

To the Open House Closer:

As Closer you may be running an Open House by yourself, or with a Greeter. If working with a Greeter you may be talking mainly with Prospects who have filled out a Registration Card, or even better a "Next Step" Form. Then you'll have the answers you need to **pre-screen fast**.

Focus your time and energy on the **most qualified Prospects**, meaning Buyers who have **5% or more** for a down payment and can afford the monthly payment. Obviously the more money they have down, the more time you spend with that Buyer.

These Open Houses can get busy very quickly. Even with a Greeter sometimes you'll need to talk with new Buyers coming in the door. Your **1st Goal** at all Open Houses is to **Identify Quality Prospects**. Your ultimate goal is to collect non-refundable option deposit checks from them.

The best way to start this process is to get all the Open House Visitors to fill out Registration Cards. If you have them complete the "Next Step" Form, that gives you the same information plus it also briefly explains the Lease Purchase Program.

When you have an Open House Greeter hopefully they are gathering most if not all of the completed Registration Cards. They should also be connecting you with any qualified Buyers based on the information they're collecting.

Your overriding goal is to Close one qualified Buyer on this home, and collect a big non-refundable option deposit. Beyond that, your next goal is to set up other qualified Buyers to buy your next home and your next one after that. Your main tools to accomplish these goals are your mouth (to talk & smile), and the Closing Meeting Script (to follow as faithfully as possible).

At the end of the Open House if you have one or more non-refundable option deposits, then you have been successful! The ultimate goal is to also have several more qualified Prospects from this Open House just waiting for your next homes.

Once you identify a good Prospect, your **2nd Goal** is to **Build Rapport**!* This is an extremely important part of your job. The more the Prospects like you, the more comfortable they will feel about moving forward and buying the home. Since you're the face of the company, you are vitally important to making a good first impression on the Buyers.

*Use the Wolffs' "Rapport Building Scripts".

Your **3rd Goal** is to **Close a Qualified Tenant Buyer** on the house! Get the completed paperwork and deposit check in your hands ASAP!

Your **4th Goal** is to **Refer the Quality Prospects** who are not interested in that particular house back to your Open House Greeter. Then instead of losing a good Prospect hopefully your Greeter can keep them excited about other properties you have or may be getting soon.

You need to focus your time and energy on the most qualified Prospects, meaning Buyers who have 5% or more down payment and can afford the monthly payment. That alone will get you the results you desire! Here's the script to get started on finding those Prospects.

GREETING NEW BUYERS

Hello, welcome to our Open House. *(shake hands with a big smile)* I'm _____, and what was your name?

(if others in party, kids too) And who's with you today?

Hi, nice to meet you, I'm _____. Great, well let me just give you one of our flyers, it tells all about the home.

(pass out flyers)

A couple things I know you'll love about the home are *(home feature #1)* , and *(home feature #2)*.

Also the best thing of all is that we're offering this home through our Lease Purchase, or Rent-to-Own Program. That means that if you qualify, then we'll give you whatever help you need to own it.

Let's start by having you just fill out one of our Registration Cards, and then you can take a look around and I (we) can answer any questions you might have.

(If Prize Drawing: Of course I'll make sure to get your card here into our prize drawing coming up at ___ o'clock).

TOP 10 TECHNIQUES FOR CREATING URGENCY
by *The* **Wolff** *Couple*

1. Use Urgent Phrases in Advertising – "New On Market!", "This One Won't Last", etc. Must keep D.O.M. (Days On Market) short.

2. Highlight 3 Attention-Grabbing Features of Home – On Zillow, Craigslist, in all Marketing Pieces

Open House Specific
(Techniques 3-10 pertain directly to Open Houses)

3. Compress the Length of Open House – Most Open Houses don't create Urgency simply because of the scheduling. The best way to create and maintain a sense of Urgency is keep the Open House to 1 Hour

4. Practice Sign Overkill – 40-50 signs, depending on area, and make sure to attach balloons too.

5. Create a Spectacle – Go Big or Go Home Signs, balloons, foil streamers, "swooper" flags, etc. You want the neighbors talking about your Open House all week, what a flurry of activity there was in the neighborhood. This builds your brand and Referral Network

6. Play Peppy Music – Silence works against you, you want activity and noise (no heavy metal or salsa dance music please)

7. Post an Energetic "Greeter" at the Door – This person is like the party host, they need to keep the energy level up with their personal enthusiasm.

8. Show a Sense of Urgency Yourself – Convery Urgency through your body language. Never stand around. Always look rushed, hurry everywhere. Stand close to people and hold eye contact. Speak in hushed and/or rushed tones. If there is nobody to talk to, you can pretend to be answering phone calls from buyers and giving directions.

9. Carry a Professional Portfolio Overflowing with Completed Applications

10. Promote Competition – Point out how serious other buyers are, and tell each one that they better get serious with a deposit check if they want this beautiful house

Lease Purchase Buyer Quick Opening Call Script
(Also Use for Answering Service Script)

Date_____ How did you hear about the home? _____

So when are you wanting to move in? _____

Who will be living in the home with you? _____

What's the most you can put down on your beautiful/nice new home?

_____

What's the most you can afford for a monthly payment? _____
Do you know what your qualifying issues are? _____
NOTES: _____

Long-Form **Lease Purchase Buyer Opening Call Script**

Date_____ **Pretty House Buyer Opening Call** *TheWolffCouple.com*

So you're calling about the home, I can help you with that.
I'm _____, and what was your Name? _____
And how did you hear about the home? _____
So when are you wanting to move in? _____ Great, now
sometimes we have more than one home available, so let me just ask
you a couple quick questions.
Who will be living in the home with you? _____
What's the most you can put down on your beautiful/nice new home?

_____

What is the most you can afford for a monthly payment? _____

*(If too low) Actually, on a lease-purchase like this it's usually a
little bit higher because you're getting the right to buy along
with your payment. So, if you had to, how much higher could
you go? _____ (If it's at least 3% of sales price)
Okay, I'm pretty sure we could work with you on that.*

And do you know what your qualifying issues are? _____

*That's okay, almost everyone we work with has some qualifying
issues. We look past that and just focus on getting you into a
great new home as quick as possible.*

(If Qualified, match them up with your "best fit" house based on
your supply & **their needs.)**

This home (our home on _____) would work great for you. **GO OVER the TOP 3-5 FEATURES of that HOME.**
Doesn't that home sound good/great? _____

(If positive response, give directions. If not, go to your next "best fit" home. If Prospect is borderline qualified, you can send them to home or your website, tell them to call you back.)

(After Giving Directions) Now it'd be a good idea to get out there as soon as possible. We've had a lot of interest in that home, and a couple people we sent out there seem very serious. Just grab a flyer and an application at the home, and get the application back to us ASAP, okay? Great, talk to you real soon then. **(Put Lead Sheet in LP Buyer Follow-Up File)**

(If Prospect has a large Option Deposit, $20,000+, you may choose to meet them at the house). You know, this home sounds like it will really work well for you. Tell you what, I/my Assistant can meet you out at the home. When can you make it over there? _____ Great, I/we'll meet you there.

NOTES:
_____
_____
_____
_____
_____
_____

Notes on Pre-Screening

Lease Purchase Buyer

You want to be sure this Buyer can eventually get qualified. You have to be sure what you are doing, and never want to set somebody up to not succeed. With credit repair or some other assistance, you have to be confident that they'll be able to qualify.

On the down payment, we're really aiming towards 10% more than 5%. Even if you have a $100,000 house, we don't want you taking less than $5,000 on anything. At the very least, take $5,000 even if the house is $80,000.

Work for Equity Buyer

You are going to ask (remarkably) not much less of a purchase price than you would for a straight Lease Purchase Buyer. If you have a $200,000 house and you fix it up really perfectly, you may be aggressive and ask $249,000 or something at the top of the market. This is a move-in ready home, and you are offering financing on a Lease Purchase.

Now if it is rough and needs work, and you think it is worth $200,000, you are going to ask around $189,000 or so. A Work for Equity Buyer will pay close to what that Lease Purchase Buyer would pay, not quite as much.

You do not want to take all their money either in the non-refundable option deposit / down payment necessarily, because they need a little bit of money to do the work on the property.

Mainly On the Answer to the Question,
"What's the most you can put down on your beautiful / nice new home?"

The money the Tenant Buyer gives you upfront is called two things, and It is important to repeat them both to the Buyer – "**Non-Refundable Option Deposit**" **&** "**Down Payment**".

Initially the money is their non-refundable option deposit, and the Tenant Buyer needs to understand that they won't get that money back if they end up moving out. Reassure them that you will be as flexible and helpful as you can be in their qualifying process.

As soon as the Buyer gets qualified their deposit becomes their down payment, and their lender will request proof from you that you received a down payment and how much. That is why it is important to always keep a record of the down payment, a picture of the check, and a bank receipt showing the check being deposited in your account.

The amount of the Buyer's non-refundable option deposit / down payment is so important to your profits and cash flow in this business that out of the 5 Main Qualifying Questions, the most important one is question #3. The vital prescreening questions you need answers to are all provided for you right here. All the other crucial checklists, instructions, and forms for your successful Open Houses can be found in our "1-Hour Sale" System.

The *"Wolffie"* Craze!

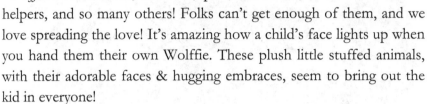

In our travels we always leave behind our beloved *"Wolffies"* to children, students, pets, celebrities, helpers, and so many others! Folks can't get enough of them, and we love spreading the love! It's amazing how a child's face lights up when you hand them their own Wolffie. These plush little stuffed animals, with their adorable faces & hugging embraces, seem to bring out the kid in everyone!

We give out FREE wonderful Wolffies worldwide, from Australia to Europe to Cuba to you-name-it! Of course part of the cost of each Wolffie goes towards saving animals for real! We love giving Wolffies and giving back, so just call us and we'll send you your very own **adorable Wolffie!** Just promise to snap a great pic somewhere cool and send it to us for our

"Wolffie Wall"!

This book has so much information, key "rubber- meets-the-road" **Strategies & Techniques you need** to make the most money as a **successful Real Estate Investor**. It may take a while to digest, you'll have to read parts over. You still won't get everything, but you'll get enough to close your 1st deal. That's where it all starts.

Of course if you find a deal, if you're on Facebook LIVE with us or on our Conference Calls or anything, we will jump in to help you. Our #1 Goal, our **Mission Statement** is to *"Help investors change their lives and the lives of their families through the application of the best real estate training anywhere."* We are committed to that, we are committed to you and your success. Any questions, any systems you are interested in, call the office anytime at **888-Rich-Now** (1-888-742-4669).

Apply the powerful knowledge here, earned from **decades of experience** in the business. We have many other proven Systems for **creating cash** and **long-term wealth** in real estate investing, all designed to speed your progress and ensure your success. You can always reach us at 888-Rich-Now, or at TheWolffCouple.com, and we love to send out **FREE Systems and Prizes** for great testimonials! We look forward to hearing all about **your success** soon!

Expect Success, Get the
Best Training, and *Take ACTION!*

CPSIA information can be obtained
at www.ICGtesting.com
Printed in the USA
LVHW080230020421
683296LV00024B/344